S&P education

GRADE 5+

Singapore MATH CHALLENGE

Terry Chew B.Sc.

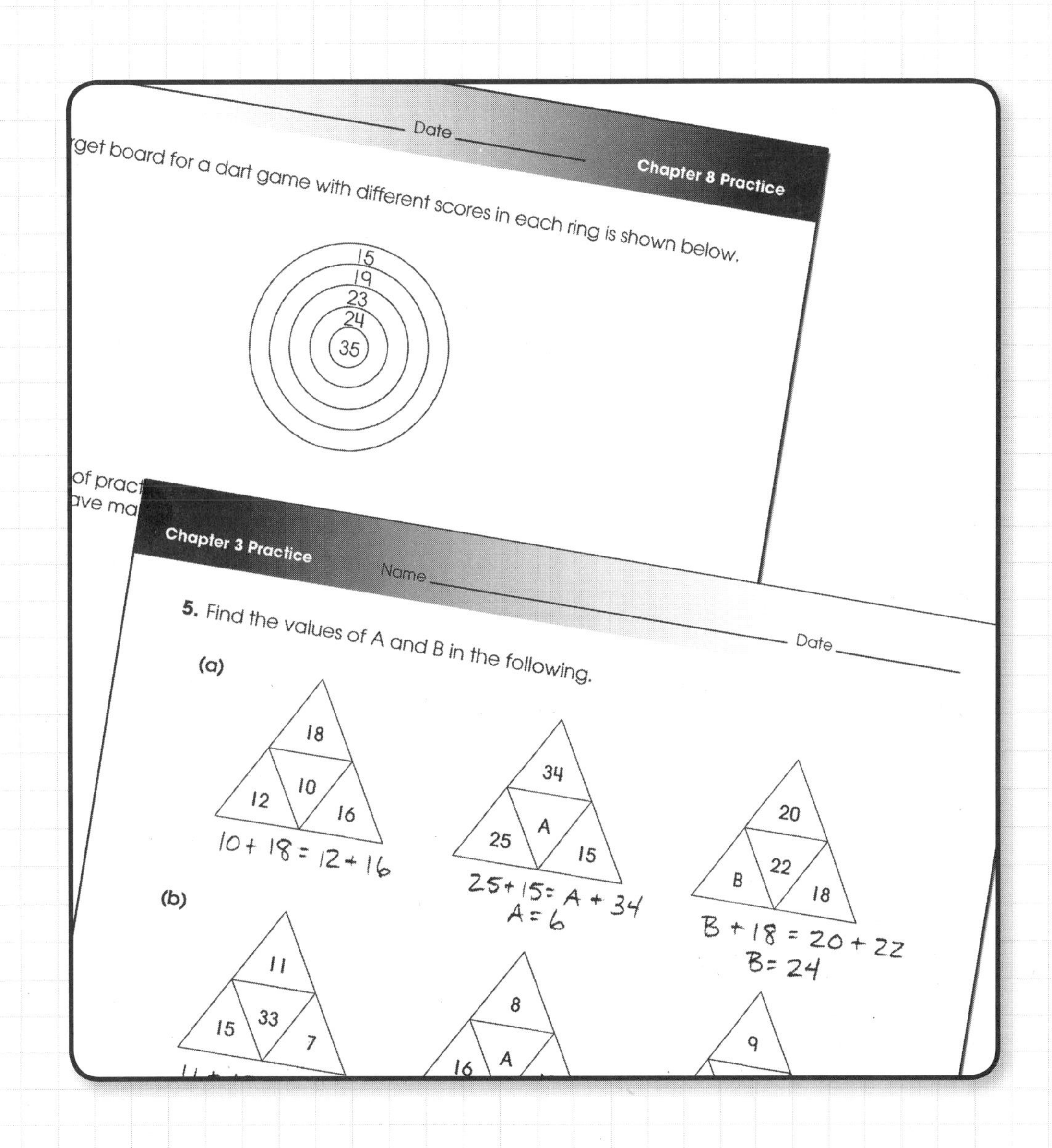
Date

Chapter 8 Practice

rget board for a dart game with different scores in each ring is shown below.

15
19
23
24
35

of pract
ave ma

Chapter 3 Practice

Name

Date

5. Find the values of A and B in the following.

(a)

18
12
10
16
10 + 18 = 12 + 16

34
25
A
15
25 + 15 = A + 34
A = 6

20
B
22
18
B + 18 = 20 + 22
B = 24

(b)

11
15
33
7

8
16
A

9

Thinking Kids®
An imprint of Carson-Dellosa Publishing
Greensboro, NC

First published in 2008 by Singapore Asia Publishers Pte. Ltd.

Thinking Kids®
An imprint of Carson-Dellosa Publishing LLC
PO Box 35665
Greensboro, NC 27425 USA

ISBN 978-1-62399-075-6
05-009177784

Letter to Parents 5

Chapter 1 The Four Operations 7

Chapter 2 Solve by Assuming 25

Chapter 3 Looking for a Pattern 36

Chapter 4 Working Backward 46

Chapter 5 Sequence with a Common Difference 58

Chapter 6 Prime Numbers 71

Chapter 7 Divisibility 93

Chapter 8 Logic 118

Chapter 9 Write Simple Equations 136

978-1-62399-075-6
Singapore Math Challenge

Chapter 10 Remainder Problems 156

Chapter 11 Average Problems 178

Chapter 12 Area 198

Chapter 13 Fractions 219

Chapter 14 Square Numbers and Value of Ones Digit 239

Chapter 15 Percentage 266

Chapter 16 Angles and Triangles 287

Solutions 310

978-1-62399-075-6
Singapore Math Challenge

In *Singapore Math Challenge*, your child will find a variety of intriguing problems and problem-solving methods. Using the step-by-step techniques will help your son or daughter develop skill and creativity as a mathematical thinker.

What is Singapore Math?

Singapore's math curriculum has been recognized worldwide for its excellence in producing students highly skilled in mathematics. Students in Singapore regularly rank at the top of the world in mathematics on the Trends in International Mathematics and Science Study (TIMSS).

The Singapore Math curriculum aims to help students develop necessary concepts and skills for everyday life and to provide students with the ability to formulate, apply, and solve problems. The Singapore Primary (Elementary) Mathematics curriculum covers fewer topics, but in greater depth. Key concepts are introduced and built-on to reinforce mathematical ideas and thinking. Skills are typically taught a full year ahead of when similar skills are taught in the United States.

Singapore Math and the Common Core State Standards

Common Core State Standards in mathematics have been adopted by most U.S. states. These standards are designed to help prepare American students for success in college and in the global twenty-first century workforce. They outline clear, consistent, and rigorous expectations for learning in math.

In developing the Common Core State Standards, experts looked at educationally high-performing nations such as Singapore to identify the best approaches to learning. Singapore math standards are frequently cited in the research used to support the Common Core standards.

Common Core State Standards have raised the bar for American students. Strategies taught in *Singapore Math Challenge* will help students meet these new expectations.

Using *Singapore Math Challenge* Books

Each chapter focuses on a challenging, age-appropriate topic and demonstrates several clever problem-solving methods. Topics in this series include:

- **Basic Concepts:**
  New ways to understand counting, telling time, odd and even numbers, place value, fractions, averaging, and prime numbers
- **Operations:**
  Tricks for solving addition, subtraction, multiplication, and division problems
- **Strategies:**
  Creative and effective approaches to problem solving, including making lists and visual models, making assumptions, comparing and replacing, and working backward
- **Classic Problems:**
  Techniques for solving problems that have interested mathematicians through the ages, including intervals, numbers in a series, speed problems, age problems, and excess-and-shortage problems
- **Logic and IQ:**
  Brain-teasing patterns, puzzles, and logic problems to strengthen mathematical thinking
- **Applied and Advanced Topics:**
  Introductions to squares and cubes, perimeter, area, angles and triangles, percentages, and writing simple algebraic equations

Students should study the examples that begin each chapter and refer back to them often as they attempt to solve the problems. Blank space is provided for working each problem. A complete worked solution for each problem can be found in the back of the book.

Invite your student to think creatively and to try different methods when solving these challenging problems. Above all, encourage your child to approach math endeavors with confidence and to think of math as a fun and fascinating journey.

978-1-62399-075-6

The Four Operations

Making computations in addition, subtraction, multiplication and division neat and simple will be the focus of this chapter.

(A) Addition and Subtraction

Important notes:

1. $a + b = b + a$
2. $a + (b - c) = a + b - c$
3. $a - (b + c) = a - b - c$
4. $a - (b - c) = a - b + c$

(B) Multiplication and Division

Important notes:

1. $a \times (b + c) = a \times b + a \times c$
2. $a \times (b - c) = a \times b - a \times c$
3. $(a + b) \div c = a \div c + b \div c$
4. $(a - b) \div c = a \div c - b \div c$
5. $a \div b \times c = a \times c \div b$
6. $a \div b \div c = a \div (b \times c)$

It is also important to know the multiplication of numbers that will give you an answer of 100 or 1,000.

$8 \times 125 = 1{,}000$
$4 \times 25 = 100$

978-1-62399-075-6
Singapore Math Challenge

(A) Addition and Subtraction

Example 1: Compute the following.

(a) $846 + 78 - 46$
$= 846 - 46 + 78$
$= 800 + 78$
$= 878$

(b) 1,000
$365 + 276 + 135 + 724$
500
$= 500 + 1{,}000$
$= 1{,}500$

(c) 1,000
$485 + 136 + 264 + 515$
400
$= 1{,}000 + 400$
$= 1{,}400$

(d) 600
$732 + 84 + 16 - 132$
100
$= 600 + 100$
$= 700$

(e) $708 + 1{,}392$
$= 700 + 8 + 1{,}392$
$= 700 + 1{,}400$
$= 2{,}100$

(f) $39 + 399 + 3{,}999$
$= 40 - 1 + 400 - 1 + 4{,}000 - 1$
$= 4{,}440 - 3$
$= 4{,}437$

Example 2: Compute the following.

(a) $527 - (186 + 327)$
200
$= 527 - 186 - 327$
$= 200 - 186$
$= 14$

(b) $565 - (388 - 135)$
700
$= 565 - 388 + 135$
$= 700 - 388$
$= 312$

978-1-62399-075-6

(c) $896 - (132 + 596)$

$= 896 - 132 - 596$ (896 − 596 = 300)

$= 300 - 132$

$= 168$

(d) $732 - (286 + 332)$

$= 732 - 286 - 332$ (732 − 332 = 400)

$= 400 - 286$

$= 114$

(e) $633 - (233 - 189)$

$= 633 - 233 + 189$

$= 400 + 189$

$= 589$

(f) $534 - (234 + 123)$

$= 534 - 234 - 123$

$= 300 - 123$

$= 177$

Example 3: Compute the following.

$100 - 99 + 98 - 97 + 96 - 95 + \ldots + 8 - 7 + 6 - 5 + 4 - 3 + 2 - 1$

$= 50 \times 1$

$= 50$

Example 4: Compute the following.

$19 + 199 + 1{,}999 + 19{,}999$

$= 20 - 1 + 200 - 1 + 2{,}000 - 1 + 20{,}000 - 1$

$= 22{,}220 - 4$

$= 22{,}216$

978-1-62399-075-6
Singapore Math Challenge

(B) Multiplication and Division

Example 1: Use a simple method to compute the following.

(a) 65×399
$= 65 \times (400 - 1)$
$= 65 \times 400 - 65 \times 1$
$= 26{,}000 - 65$
$= 25{,}935$

(b) $25 \times 16 \times 125$
$= 25 \times 2 \times 8 \times 125$
$= 50 \times 1{,}000$
$= 50{,}000$

(c) 198×36
$= (200 - 2) \times 36$
$= 200 \times 36 - 2 \times 36$
$= 7{,}200 - 72$
$= 7{,}128$

(d) $25 \times 32 \times 125 \times 35$
$= 25 \times 4 \times 8 \times 125 \times 35$
$= 100 \times 1{,}000 \times 35$
$= 3{,}500{,}000$

(e) 600×99
$= 600 \times (100 - 1)$
$= 60{,}000 - 600$
$= 59{,}400$

(f) $25 \times 96 \times 125$
$= 25 \times 12 \times 8 \times 125$
$= 25 \times 4 \times 3 \times 1{,}000$
$= 100 \times 3 \times 1{,}000$
$= 3 \times 100{,}000$
$= 300{,}000$

Example 2: Use a simple method to compute the following.

(a) $37 \times 88 + 37 \times 12$
$= 37 \times (88 + 12)$
$= 37 \times 100$
$= 3{,}700$

(b) $18 \times 114 - 18 \times 14$
$= 18 \times (114 - 14)$
$= 18 \times 100$
$= 1{,}800$

(c) $42 \times 75 + 42 \times 25$
$= 42 \times (75 + 25)$
$= 42 \times 100$
$= 4{,}200$

(d) $33 \times 126 - 33 \times 26$
$= 33 \times (126 - 26)$
$= 33 \times 100$
$= 3{,}300$

Example 3: Use a simple method to compute the following.

(a) $210 \div (5 \times 6)$
$= 210 \div 5 \div 6$
$= 42 \div 6$
$= 7$

(b) $748 \div (17 \times 11)$
$= 748 \div 11 \div 17$
$= 68 \div 17$
$= 4$

(c) $4{,}000 \div 125 \div 8$
$= 4{,}000 \div (125 \times 8)$
$= 4{,}000 \div 1{,}000$
$= 4$

(d) $56 \times 198 \div 11 \div 7$
$= 198 \div 11 \times 56 \div 7$
$= 18 \times 8$
$= 144$

978-1-62399-075-6
Singapore Math Challenge

 Name ______________________ Date ____________

Example 4: Use a simple method to compute the following.

(a) $333 \times 222 \div 666$
$= 333 \times 2 \times 111 \div 666$
$= 666 \times 111 \div 666$
$= 111$

(b) $4{,}444 \times 2{,}222 \div 8{,}888$
$= 4{,}444 \times 2 \times 1{,}111 \times 8{,}888$
$= 8{,}888 \times 1{,}111 \div 8{,}888$
$= 1{,}111$

(c) $454{,}545{,}450 \div 9 \div 5$
$= 454{,}545{,}450 \div (9 \times 5)$
$= 454{,}545{,}450 \div 45$
$= 10{,}101{,}010$

(d) $999 + 999 \times 999$
$= 999 \times (1 + 999)$
$= 999 \times 1{,}000$
$= 999{,}000$

978-1-62399-075-6

1. Compute the following.

(a) 456 + 88 − 56

(b) 374 + 56 − 74

356

(c) 3,035 − 998 − 997

3035
−1995
1040

(d) 999 + 3 + 98 + 998 + 3 + 9

1000 100 1000 10

2110

(e) 636 − 567 − 99 + 367

636
− 200
436

337

(f) 5,034 − 997 − 998 − 999

5034
−2994
2040

(g) 123 + 456 + 544 + 877

(h) 3,456 + 4,567 + 6,544 + 5,433

4567
+5433
10000

978-1-62399-075-6
Singapore Math Challenge

2. Compute the following.

(a) 2,208 – (208 + 139)

(b) 733 – (33 + 320)

700

380

(c) 1,306 – (406 – 258)

900

1158

(d) 945 + (372 – 245) – 172

700 + 200

978-1-62399-075-6

(e) 644 – (243 – 156) + 143

644 – (100 – 156)

700

(f) 717 – (617 – 225)

100

325

(g) 937 – (137 + 185) + 85

937 – (137 + 100)

700

(h) 1,732 – (732 – 257)

1000

1257

(i) 788 – (288 + 546) + 346

788 – (288 + 200)

978-1-62399-075-6
Singapore Math Challenge

3. Compute the following.

(a) 37 + 397 + 3,997 + 39,997

(b) 298 + 2,998 + 29,998 + 299,998

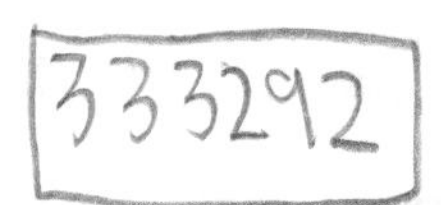

(c) 9 + 99 + 999 + 9,999 + 99,999

978-1-62399-075-6

4. Compute the following.

(a) $(2 + 4 + 6 + \ldots + 2{,}006) - (1 + 3 + 5 + \ldots + 2{,}005)$

1003

(b) $88 - 87 + 86 - 85 + \ldots + 4 - 3 + 2 - 1$

44

(c) $100 - 98 + 96 - 94 + \ldots + 8 - 6 + 4 - 2$

50

978-1-62399-075-6

5. Compute the following.

(a) $360 - 357 + 354 - 351 + \ldots + 300 - 297$

33

(b) $2{,}006 - 1 - 2 - 3 - 4 - \ldots - 48 - 49 - 50$

51 × 25 = 255 + 102(0) = 1275

2006 − 1275 = 731

(c) $280 - 276 + 272 - 268 + \ldots + 200 - 196$

44

978-1-62399-075-6
Singapore Math Challenge

6. Use a simple method to compute the following.

(a) $56 \times 8 + 88 \times 4$

100
8
800

(b) $1{,}600 \div 25$

64

(c) $56 \times 33 + 44 \times 33$

100
33
3300

(d) $73 \times 12 + 27 \times 12$

1200

(e) 198×56

198
× 56
1188
9900
11088

(f) $5 \times 64 \times 25 \times 125 \times 97$

1600

97
× 5
485

485
× 200000
97000000

(g) $64 \times 25 \times 125 \times 16$

1600
× 2000
3200000

(h) $16{,}000 \div 25$

640

978-1-62399-075-6
Singapore Math Challenge

(i) $125 \times 25 \times 5 \times 64$

(j) $101 \times 1{,}001 - 101$

7. Use a simple method to compute the following.

(a) $5{,}000 \div 8 \div 125$

(b) $6{,}000 \div 25 \div 4$

(c) $30{,}000 \div 2 \div 8 \div 5 \div 125$

(d) $16{,}000 \div 125 \div 4 \div 8$

978-1-62399-075-6

(e) 32,000 ÷ 125

256

(f) 5,300 ÷ 25

212

(g) 1,400 ÷ 25

56

(h) 72,000 ÷ 125

288
× 2
576

8. Use a simple method to compute the following.

(a) 89 × 11 + 11 × 11

1100

(b) 29 × 8 + 42 × 4

400

(c) 58 × 8 + 84 × 4

100
8
800

(d) 58 × 30 + 84 × 15

3000

(e) $63 \times 6 + 74 \times 3$

(f) $74 \times 6 + 152 \times 3$

900

(g) $44 \times 4 + 78 \times 8$

(h) $56 \times 16 + 72 \times 32$

3200

9. Use a simple method to compute the following.

(a) $35 \times 128 - 28 \times 35$

3500

(b) $46 \times 234 - 134 \times 46$

4600

(c) $287 \times 12 - 187 \times 12$

1200

(d) $897 \times 30 - 297 \times 30$

18000

(e) $69 \times 36 - 38 \times 18$

1800

(f) $74 \times 54 - 48 \times 27$

2700

(g) $132 \times 36 - 196 \times 12$

396

200
12

2400

(h) $156 \times 48 - 124 \times 12$

624

500
× 12

6000

978-1-62399-075-6
Singapore Math Challenge

10. Use a simple method to compute the following.

(a) 3,333 × 3,333 ÷ 9,999

(b) 2,222 × 9,999 ÷ 3,333

6666

(c) 99,999 × 88,888 ÷ 11,111

88888
× 9

72
72
72
72
72
799992

(d) 6,666 × 8 + 4,444 × 13

2222 × 24 + 2222 × 26

2222 × 50

978-1-62399-075-6
Singapore Math Challenge

Solve by Assuming

Problems introduced in this chapter are most commonly solved using tables, which can be tedious at times. Instead, we attempt to solve problems of this nature by asking, "If all were ...."

Example 1: A farmer has 36 chickens and rabbits. There are 96 legs altogether. How many chickens does the farmer have?
How many rabbits does the farmer have?

Solution:

Method 1: Solve by Assuming

If all are chickens, there will be 36 × 2 = 72 legs.

96 – 72 = 24
All the rabbits have been counted as if they are chickens.

4 – 2 = 2
The difference in the number of legs between a chicken and a rabbit is 2.

24 ÷ 2 = 12 rabbits
36 – 12 = 24 chickens

Method 2: Solve by Assuming
If all are rabbits, there will be 36 × 4 = 144 legs.

144 – 96 = 48
There will be an extra 48 legs.

4 – 2 = 2
The difference in the number of legs between a rabbit and a chicken is 2.

48 ÷ 2 = 24 chickens
36 – 24 = 12 rabbits
The farmer has 24 chickens and 12 rabbits.

978-1-62399-075-6

 Name ______ Date ______

Example 2: A cashier collected \$312 from the sale of 50 tickets. An adult ticket cost \$8. A child ticket cost \$4. How many tickets of each type did the cashier sell?

Solution:

Method 1: Solve by Assuming

If all were adult tickets, 50 × \$8 = \$400 would be collected.

\$400 – \$312 = \$88
There would be an extra \$88.

\$8 – \$4 = \$4
The price difference between an adult ticket and a child ticket was \$4.

\$88 ÷ \$4 = 22 child tickets
50 – 22 = 28 adult tickets

Method 2: Solve by Assuming
If all were child tickets, 50 × \$4 = \$200 would be collected.

\$312 – \$200 = \$112
There would be a shortfall of \$112.

\$8 – \$4 = \$4
The price difference between an adult ticket and a child ticket was \$4.

\$112 ÷ \$4 = 28 adult tickets
50 – 28 = 22 child tickets
The cashier sold 28 adult tickets and 22 child tickets.

978-1-62399-075-6
Singapore Math Challenge

Example 3: There are 30 questions in a math competition. 5 points are awarded for each correct answer and 2 points are deducted for each incorrect answer. If Colin scores 122 points for the math competition, how many incorrect answers does he give?

Solution:

If Colin gets all the answers correct, he will get $30 \times 5 = 150$ points.

$150 - 122 = 28$
There is an extra 28 points.

$5 + 2 = 7$
The difference in points between a correct answer and an incorrect answer is 7 points.

$28 \div 7 = 4$ incorrect answers
He gives 4 incorrect answers.

978-1-62399-075-6
Singapore Math Challenge

Example 4: 5 similar basketballs and 6 similar volleyballs cost \$325. A basketball costs \$10 more than a volleyball. What is the price of a basketball?

Solution:

Method 1: Solve by Assuming

\$325 + 6 × \$10 = \$385
If all are basketballs, the total price will be \$385.

5 + 6 = 11
The total number of basketballs will then be 11.

385 ÷ 11 = \$35

Method 2: Solve by Assuming

\$325 – 5 × \$10 = \$275
If all are volleyballs, the total price will be \$275.

5 + 6 = 11
The total number of volleyballs will then be 11.

\$275 ÷ 11 = \$25
\$25 + \$10 = \$35

The price of a basketball is \$35.

978-1-62399-075-6

Example 5: Mr. Brannon has 58 two-dollar, five-dollar and ten-dollar bills altogether in his wallet. The total value of these bills is $322. The number of two-dollar and ten-dollar bills is the same. How many bills of different denominations does he have?

Solution:

We "create" a new denomination, which is a ($10 + $2) ÷ 2 = $6 bill.

Method 1: Solve by Assuming
If all are six-dollar bills, the total value will be 58 × $6 = $348.

$348 – $322 = $26
The difference in the total value of all the bills is $26.

$6 – $5 = $1
The difference in value between a six-dollar bill and a five-dollar bill is $1.

$26 ÷ $1 = 26 five-dollar bills
58 – 26 = 32 two-dollar and ten-dollar bills
32 ÷ 2 = 16 for each two-dollar and ten-dollar bill

Method 2: Solve by Assuming
If all are five-dollar bills, the total value will be 58 × $5 = $290.

$322 – $290 = $32
The difference in the total value of all the bills is $32.

$6 – $5 = $1
$32 ÷ $1 = 32 two-dollar and ten-dollar bills
32 ÷ 2 = 16 for each two-dollar and ten-dollar bill
58 – 32 = 26 five-dollar bills

He has 16 two-dollar bills, 26 five-dollar bills and 16 ten-dollar bills.

978-1-62399-075-6
Singapore Math Challenge

 Name ______________________ Date __________

1. A farmer has 45 chickens and rabbits. There are 140 legs altogether. How many chickens does the farmer have? How many rabbits does the farmer have?

90 50

25 20
rabbits Chickens

2. A spider has 8 legs. A dragonfly has 6 legs. 28 spiders and dragonflies have 200 legs altogether. How many spiders are there? How many dragonflies are there?

28
×6
168

168 32

12 16
flies spiders

978-1-62399-075-6

3. Andy spent $55 in all to purchase 20 two-dollar and five-dollar toys. How many two-dollar toys did he buy? How many five-dollar toys did he buy?

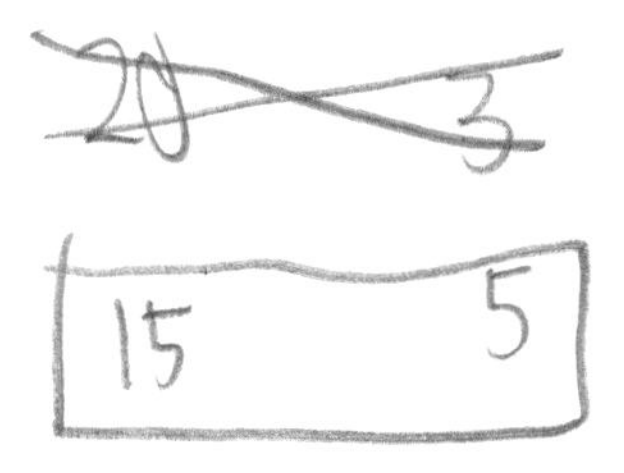

4. There are 40 cars and motorcycles in a park. There are 116 wheels altogether. How many cars are there? How many motorcycles are there?

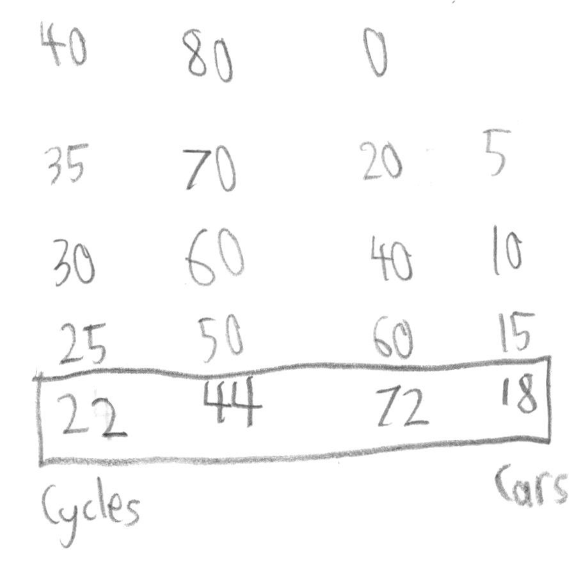

978-1-62399-075-6
Singapore Math Challenge

 Name ______________________ Date __________

5. An adult ticket to a concert cost \$35 and a food ticket cost \$18. Mr. Walter paid \$598 in all for 20 such tickets. How many adult tickets did he buy? How many food tickets did he buy?

598 − 360 = 238   17

17)238 = 14

14 Concert   6 food

6. Jeff has 20 five-dollar and ten-dollar bills in his wallet. The total value of these bills is \$125. How many bills of each denomination does he have?

20 100 0

15 75 50 5

\$5   \$10

7. A science quiz consists of 15 questions. 2 points are awarded for every correct answer and 1 point is deducted for every wrong answer. Kelly scores 21 points on the science quiz. How many questions does she answer correctly?

8. There are 30 questions in a math competition. 5 points are awarded for each question answered correctly and 3 points are deducted for each wrong answer. Rena scores 126 points for the math competition. How many questions does she get wrong?

978-1-62399-075-6

9. A math quiz consists of 30 questions. The first 20 questions are worth 4 points each. The last 10 questions are worth 7 points each. No points will be deducted for each wrong answer. Justin scores 124 points on the math quiz. How many of the first 20 questions and how many of the last 10 questions does he answer incorrectly?

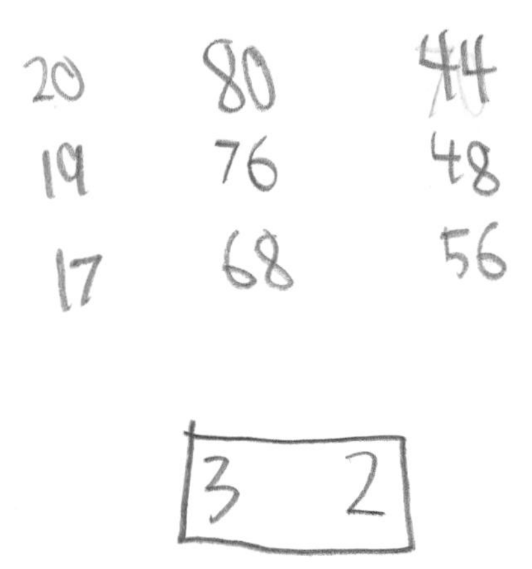

10. Mr. George spent $375 in all for 5 similar tables and 6 similar chairs. Each table cost $20 more than each chair. What was the price of a table? What was the price of a chair?

978-1-62399-075-6
Singapore Math Challenge

11. Mr. Gretzky spent $390 on 5 similar basketballs and 4 similar volleyballs. Each basketball cost $15 more than each volleyball.
What was the price of a basketball and the price of a volleyball?

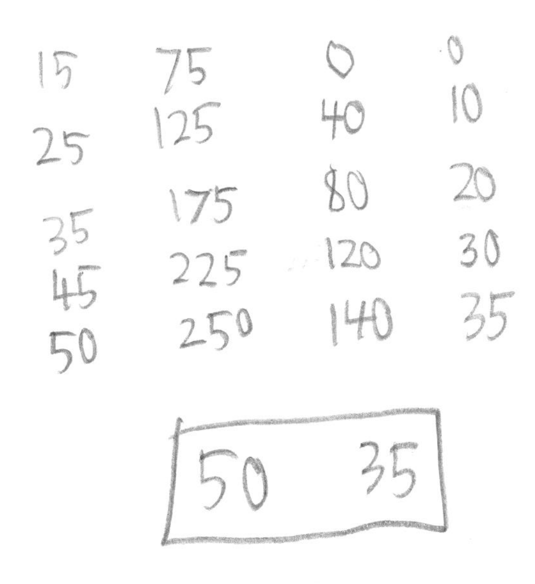

12. Wayne has 20 bills. The denominations are $2, $5 and $10. The number of $2 bills and $10 bills is the same. The total value of these bills is $110. How many bills of each denomination does he have?

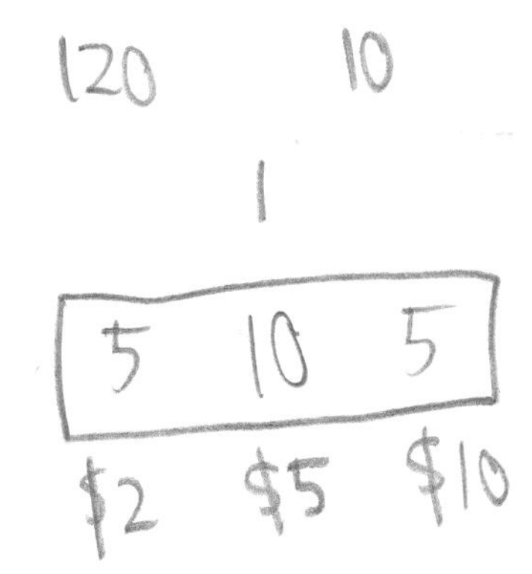

Looking for a Pattern

1. Complete the number patterns.

(a) 1, 2, 4, 8, 16, (32), (64), ⋯

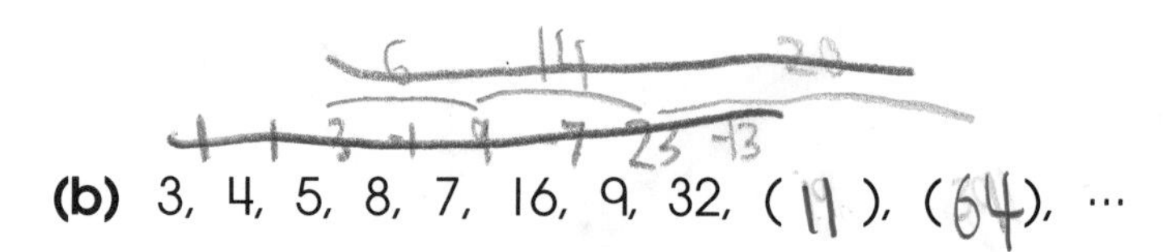

(b) 3, 4, 5, 8, 7, 16, 9, 32, (11), (64), ⋯

(c) 0, 3, 8, 15, 24, (35), (48), 63, ⋯

(d) 6, 1, 8, 3, 10, 5, 12, 7, (14), (9), ⋯

(e) 2, 3, 5, (8), (12), 17, (23), ⋯

(f) 3, 5, 6, 10, (9), 15, (12), (20), ⋯

4 8 16 32 64 128

(g) 7, 11, 19, (35), 67, (131), (259), ⋯

(h) 8, 12, 20, (32), (48), (68), ⋯

978-1-62399-075-6
Singapore Math Challenge

2. What are the missing numbers in the number patterns below?

(a)

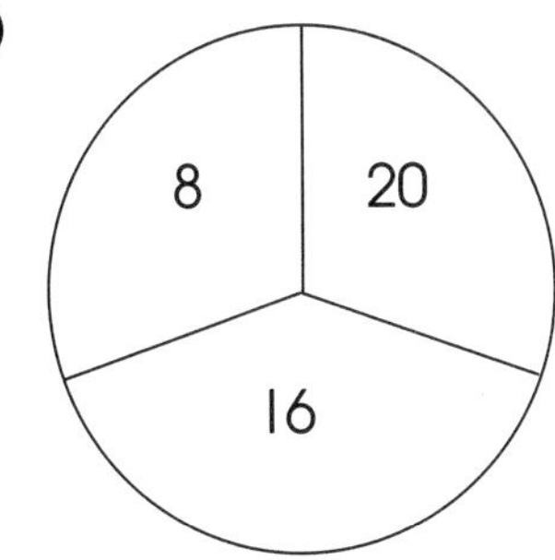

18 | 40 | 36

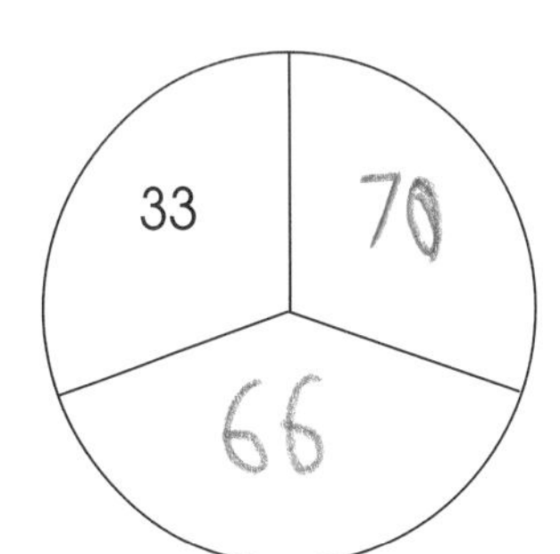

(b)

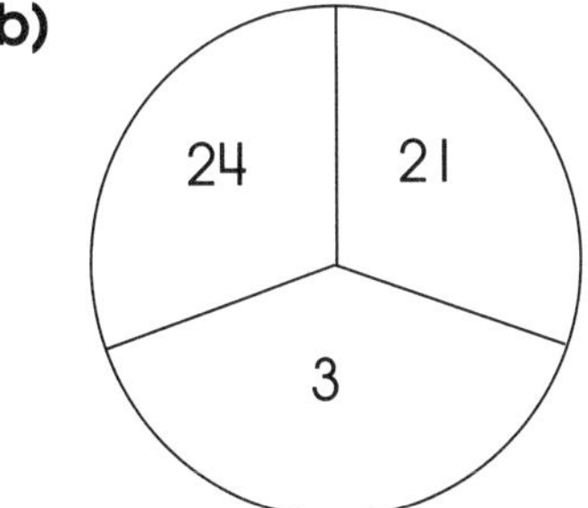

66 | 63 | 9

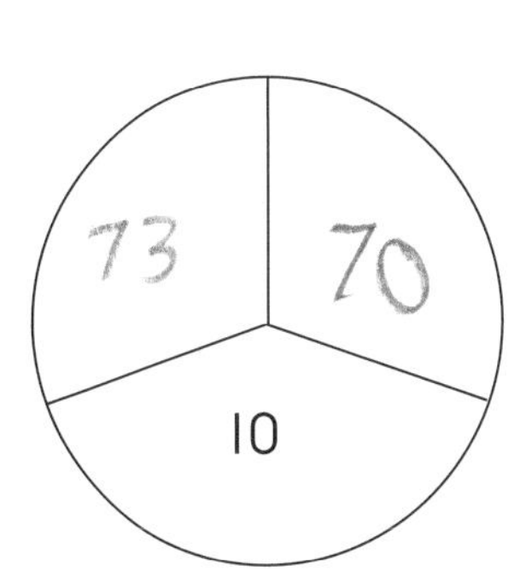

(c)

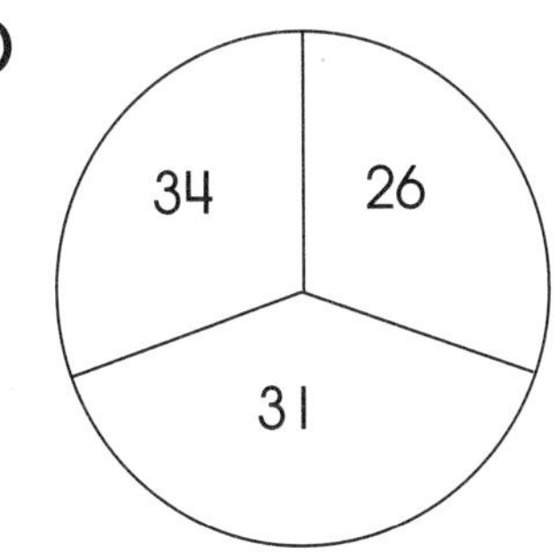

42 | 34 | 39

55 | 47 | 52

978-1-62399-075-6
Singapore Math Challenge

3. Find the missing numbers.

$1 \times 9 + 2 = 11$

$12 \times 9 + 3 = 111$

$123 \times 9 + 4 = 1,111$

$1,234 \times 9 + (\ 5\ ) = 11,111$

$(\ 12345\ ) \times 9 + 6 = 111,111$

$123,456 \times 9 + 7 = 1,111,111$

$1,234,567 \times 9 + 8 = (\ 11111111\ )$

4. Find the 4th, 7th and 8th terms in the number sequence below.

4 9 16 25 36 49 64

1, 5, 14, (30), 55, 91, (140), (204), ...

5. Find the values of A and B in the following.

(a)

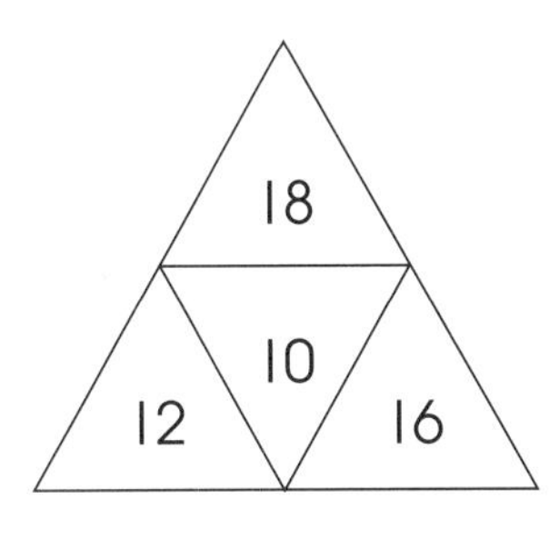

34
A
25
15

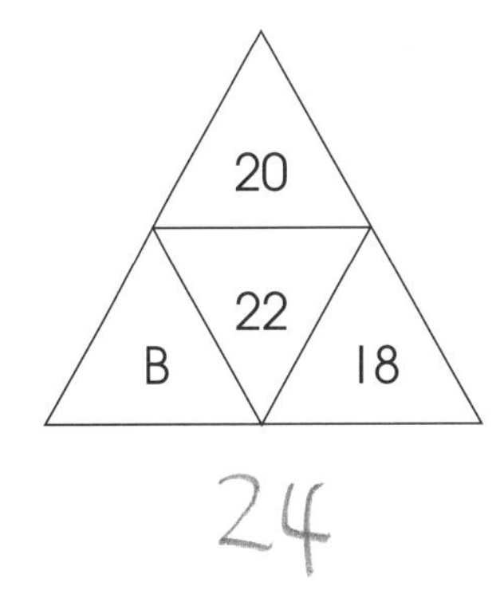

(b)

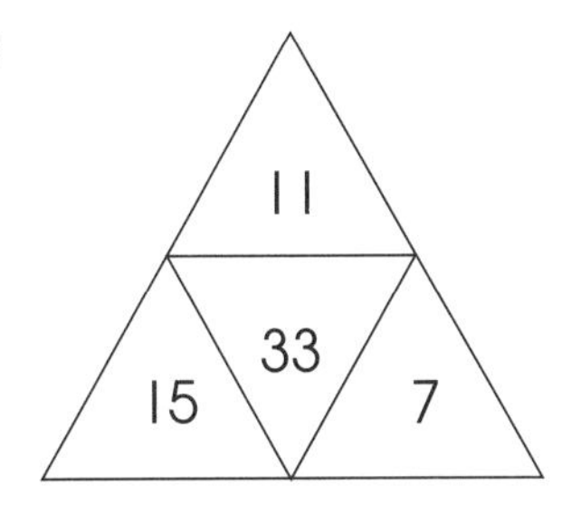

8
A
16
10

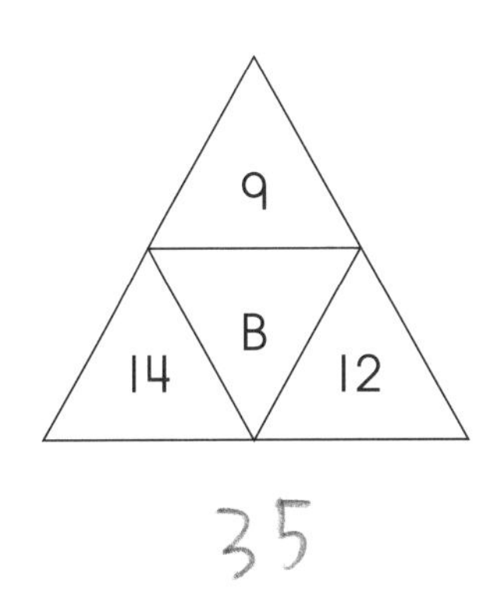

(c)

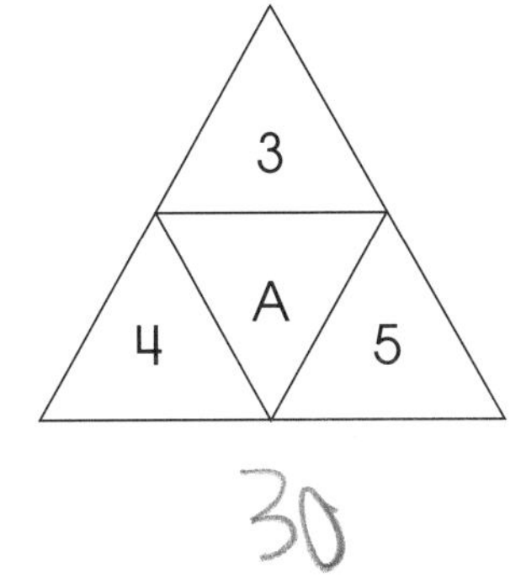

8
12
3
1

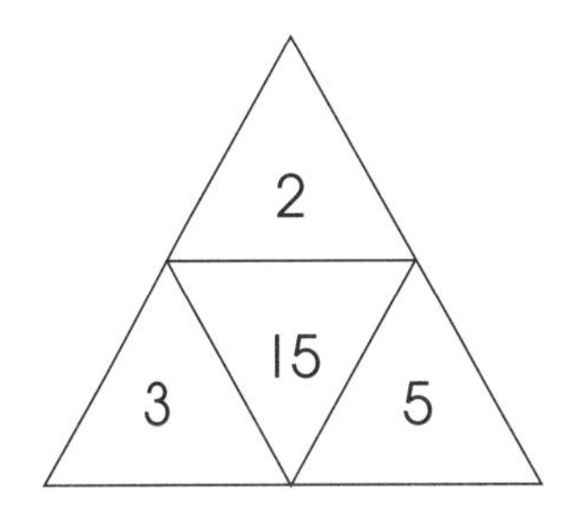

6. Find the missing numbers.

11 × 11 = 121

111 × 111 = 12,321

1,111 × 1,111 = 1,234,321

(11111) × 11,111 = 123,454,321

111,111 × 111,111 = (12345654321)

1,111,111 × (1111111) = 1,234,567,654,321

11,111,111 × 11,111,111 = (123456787654321)

7. Find the missing numbers.

8,547 × 13 = 111,111
8,547 × 26 = 222,222
8,547 × (78) = 666,666
8,547 × 39 = 333,333
8,547 × (104) = 888,888
8,547 × (117) = 999,999
8,547 × 91 = 777,777
8,547 × 65 = (555555)

978-1-62399-075-6
Singapore Math Challenge

8. Complete the number patterns.

(a) 2, 3, 5, 8, 13, 21, (34), (55), ...

(b) 1, 4, 9, 16, (25), (36), (49), ...

(c) 6, 3, 8, 5, 10, (7), (12), (9), ...

(d) 9, 11, 15, 21, (29), 39, (51), (65), ...

(e) 8, 20, 44, 92, (188), (380), (764), ...

(f) 5, 17, 53, 161, (485), (1457), 4,373, ...

(g) 2, 25, 140, 715, (3590), 17,965, ...

(h) 3, 18, 78, (318), (1278), 5,118, ...

978-1-62399-075-6
Singapore Math Challenge

9. What are the numbers in the eighth group in the pattern below?

(1, 3, 6) (2, 6, 9) (3, 9, 12) ...

(8, 24, 27)

10. What are the numbers in the twelfth group in the pattern below?

(1, 4, 8) (2, 8, 12) (3, 12, 16) ...

(x, 2x,

(12, 48, 52)

11. Find the sum of the numbers in the 50th group in the pattern below.

(1, 1, 2) (2, 4, 12) (3, 9, 36) ...

$(x, x^2, x^3 + x^2)$

(50, 2500, 127500)

12. Complete the number pattern.

$1 + 3 = 4 = 2 \times 2$

$1 + 3 + 5 = 9 = 3 \times 3$

$1 + 3 + 5 + 7 = 16 = 4 \times 4$

$(1+3+5+7+9) = (25) = 5 \times 5$

$1 + 3 + 5 + 7 + 9 + 11 = 36 = (6 \times 6)$

978-1-62399-075-6
Singapore Math Challenge

13. What is the 12th term in the number pattern below?

3, 8, 15, 24, 35, 48, 63, ...

5 7 9 11 13 15 17 19 21 23 25

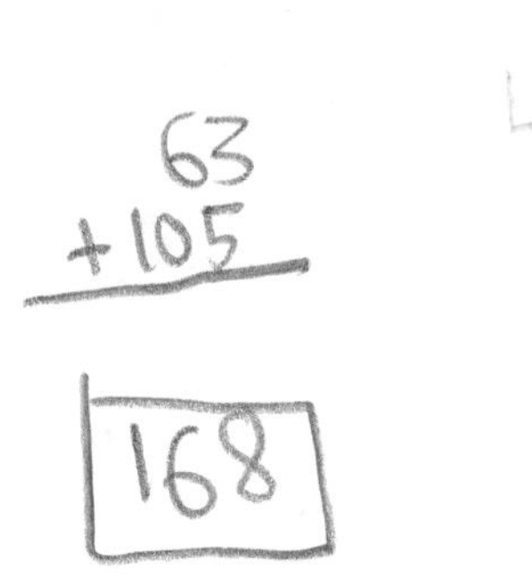

14. In the number pattern below, in which row is 2,007?

1

2 3

4 5 6

7 8 9 10

11 12 13 14 15

... ...

... ...

15 120

15. In the number pattern below, the third number is the sum of the first two numbers. The fourth number is the sum of the previous two consecutive numbers and so on. What is the second number?

3, ( ), ( ), ( ), ( ), 54, ...

16. In the number pattern below, which term will be $\frac{15}{30}$?

$\frac{1}{1}, \frac{1}{2}, \frac{2}{2}, \frac{1}{3}, \frac{2}{3}, \frac{3}{3}, \frac{1}{4}, \frac{2}{4}, \frac{3}{4}, \frac{4}{4}, \ldots$

978-1-62399-075-6
Singapore Math Challenge

 Name ____________________ Date __________

Working Backward

Parentheses are important in complex number sentences as they show the order of operations. Below shows the law of parentheses in the order of operations.

Ordinary parentheses	( )	: First priority
Square brackets	( )	: Second priority
Braces	{ }	: Third priority

Example 1: Find the missing number.

$$7 \times \square \div 11 \times 45 = 4{,}095$$

Solution:

$$\begin{aligned} \square &= 4{,}095 \div 45 \times 11 \div 7 \\ &= 91 \times 11 \div 7 \\ &= 13 \times 11 \\ &= 143 \end{aligned}$$

978-1-62399-075-6
Singapore Math Challenge

Example 2: At a supermarket sale, 2 more than half of the number of apples were taken out from a box. Later, 2 fewer than half of the remaining number of apples were taken out again. If 20 apples were left in the box, how many apples were there at first?

Solution:

(?) —÷ 2→ [38] —− 2→ [36] —÷ 2→ [18] —+ 2→ 20

(76) ←× 2— [38] ←+ 2— [36] ←× 2— [18] ←− 2— 20

 Name ______________________ Date ____________

1. Find the missing number.

$(12 + 11 \times \square) \div 12 = 12$

2. Find the missing number.

$\left(\frac{1 + \square}{7} + 4\right) \div 8 = \frac{4}{7}$

$\frac{32}{7} = \left(\frac{1+x}{7} + 4\right)$

978-1-62399-075-6

3. Find the missing number.

$$\left((\square + 4) \times 8\right) \div 12 = 40$$

4. Find the missing number.

$$\left(\frac{1 + \square}{9} + 3\right) \div 4 = \frac{8}{9}$$

$\frac{32}{9} = ($

978-1-62399-075-6

5. 6 is first subtracted from a number. The difference is then multiplied by 6. The product is added to 6. Lastly, the sum is divided by 6. The answer is 6. What is the value of this number?

6
36
30
5
11

6. A number is added to 6. The sum is then multiplied by 3. The product is divided by 8. 8 is then subtracted from the quotient.
The answer is 1. Find the number.

1
9
72
24
18

7. David asked his grandfather about his age. His grandfather replied, "You may add my age to 42 and divide the sum by 3. You then subtract 36 from the quotient. Then, you multiply the difference by 25 and the result will be 100." Help David solve this math puzzle to find his grandfather's age.

8. ABC Megamart sold 4 sacks more than half its sacks of rice on the first day of a week. It sold 3 sacks fewer than half of the remaining sacks of rice on the second day. ABC Megamart ordered another 30 sacks of rice on the third day. It had a total stock of 50 sacks then. How many sacks of rice did ABC Megamart have at first?

978-1-62399-075-6

9. An army of ants was migrating. The ants moved 120 grams less than half of their food on their first trip. On their second trip, they managed to move 100 g more than half of the remaining amount of food. They moved 480 g of food on their third trip. 280 g of food was still unmoved. How much food did the army of ants have at first?

280
760
1240
~~1740~~

10. ABC Telco sold 20 more than half its cell phone inventory in January. It sold 15 more than half the remaining number of cell phones in February. It had 75 cell phones left in March before any purchase was made. How many cell phones did ABC Telco carry at first?

11. A subtrahend is the number being subtracted in a subtraction problem. Robert misread the digit 1 in the ones place of the subtrahend as 7 and the digit 7 in the tens place of the subtrahend as 1. The difference in the subtraction then became 222. What would be the actual difference if he had read the numbers correctly?

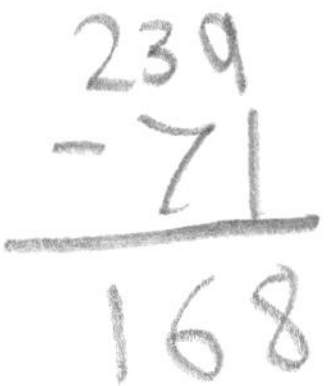

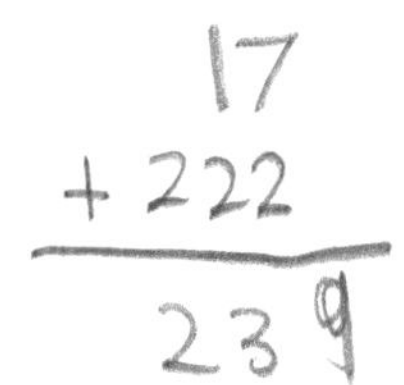

12. There were some marbles in a bag. Jeff took half of the marbles out of the bag. He then put 1 marble back into the bag. He repeated this process five times. There were 3 marbles left in the bag at the end. How many marbles were there in the bag at first?

978-1-62399-075-6
Singapore Math Challenge

13. Alison, Beatrice and Chloe each had some books. Alison gave Beatrice and Chloe some books that doubled the number of books they had at first. Beatrice then gave some books to Alison and Chloe that doubled the number of books they had. Lastly, Chloe gave Alison and Beatrice some books that doubled the number of books they had. Each of them had 32 books at the end. How many books did each of them have at first?

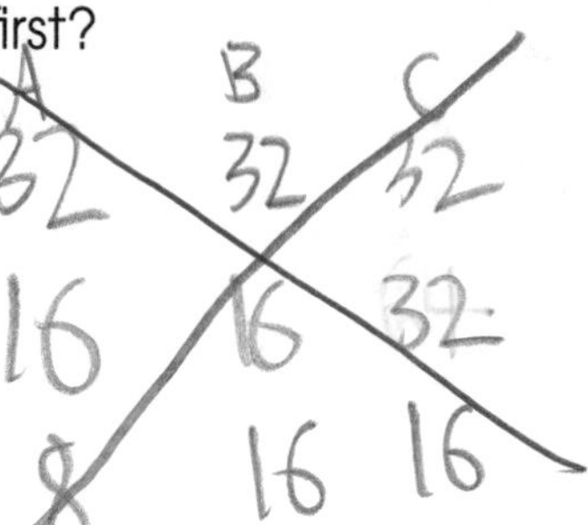

978-1-62399-075-6
Singapore Math Challenge

14. A number of commuters were on a bus when it started its journey from the bus station. At the first bus stop, $\frac{1}{7}$ of the commuters got off. At the second bus stop, $\frac{1}{6}$ of the remaining commuters got off, ... At the sixth bus stop, half the number of commuters got off and the bus was left with only 4 commuters. How many commuters boarded the bus at the bus station?

$\frac{1}{7}$ $\frac{1}{6}$ $\frac{1}{5}$ $\frac{1}{4}$ $\frac{1}{3}$ $\frac{1}{2}$

4
8
12
16
20
24
28

978-1-62399-075-6
Singapore Math Challenge

15. Sean was playing with his bubble wand. His bubble wand could eject 100 bubbles at once. Half of the bubbles would burst within one minute. $\frac{1}{4}$ of the original number of the bubbles would survive for 2 minutes. Only 2% of the original number of bubbles would make it to the end of 3 minutes. All the bubbles would burst at the 4th minute. If Sean blew the bubble wand every minute, how many bubbles were there altogether at the 10th minute?

978-1-62399-075-6
Singapore Math Challenge

16. I have some beads. When I divide all the beads into 4 equal groups, 1 bead is left. When I divide one such group into 4 equal groups again, the remainder will still be 1. When I split one such group into 4 equal groups again, the remainder is still 1. What is the minimum number of beads I have?

978-1-62399-075-6
Singapore Math Challenge

Sequence with a Common Difference

In a number sequence where the difference between every two terms is the same, we can use the formulas shown below.

n^{th} term = first term + (number of terms − 1) × d where d is the common difference

number of terms in a number sequence = (last term − first term) ÷ d + 1 where d is the common difference

sum of a sequence = (last term + first term) × number of terms ÷ 2

978-1-62399-075-6
Singapore Math Challenge

Example 1: Given the number sequence, 1, 4, 7, 10, 13, ...
Find the 15th term of the number sequence. Which term is number 55?

Solution:

$d = 4 - 1 = 7 - 4 = 10 - 7 = 13 - 10 = 3$

$$\begin{aligned} 15^{th} \text{ term} &= \text{first term} + (15 - 1) \times d \\ &= 1 + 14 \times 3 \\ &= 1 + 42 = 43 \end{aligned}$$

To find the term of number 55,

Method 1:

$$\begin{aligned} (55 - 1) \div 3 + 1 &= 54 \div 3 + 1 \\ &= 18 + 1 \\ &= 19 \end{aligned}$$

Method 2:

$$\begin{aligned} 1 + (n - 1) \times 3 &= 55 \\ 1 + 3n - 3 &= 55 \\ 3n - 2 &= 55 \\ 3n &= 55 + 2 = 57 \\ n &= 57 \div 3 = 19 \end{aligned}$$

The 15th term of the number sequence is 43. Number 55 is the 19th term.

978-1-62399-075-6
Singapore Math Challenge

Example 2: Find the 20th term of the number sequence, 1, 6, 11, 16, 21, ...
Which term is number 136?

Solution:

$d = 6 - 1 = 11 - 6 = 16 - 11 = 21 - 16 = 5$

20th term $= 1 + (20 - 1) \times 5 = 1 + 19 \times 5$
$= 96$

To find the term of number 136,

Method 1: $(136 - 1) \div 5 + 1 = 135 \div 5 + 1$
$= 28$

Method 2:

$1 + (n - 1) \times 5 = 136$
$1 + 5n - 5 = 136$
$5n = 136 + 5 - 1 = 140$
$n = 140 \div 5 = 28$

The 20th term of the number sequence is 96. Number 136 is the 28th term.

Example 3: Find the 32nd term of the number sequence, 3, 7, 11, 15, 19, ...
Which term is number 239?

Solution:

$d = 7 - 3 = 11 - 7 = 15 - 11 = 19 - 15 = 4$

$3 + (32 - 1) \times 4 = 3 + 124$
$= 127$

To find the term of number 239,

Method 1: $(239 - 3) \div 4 + 1 = 236 \div 4 + 1$
$= 60$

Method 2: $3 + (n - 1) \times 4 = 239$
$3 + 4n - 4 = 239$
$4n = 239 + 4 - 3 = 240$
$n = 240 \div 4 = 60$

The 32nd term of the number sequence is 127. Number 239 is the 60th term.

978-1-62399-075-6
Singapore Math Challenge

Example 4: The 4th term of a number sequence with a common difference is 16. The 8th term is 28. Find the 12th term.

Solution:

16, ..., ..., ..., 28
4th 8th

$d = (28 - 16) \div (8 - 4) = 12 \div 4 = 3$

16, 19, 22, 25, 28, 31, 34, 37, 40, ...

The 12th term is 40.

Example 5: The 1st term of a number sequence with a common difference is 3. The 51st term is 203. Find the 100th term.

Solution:

3, ..., ..., ..., 203
1st 51st

$d = (203 - 3) \div (51 - 1) = 200 \div 50 = 4$

$3 + (100 - 1) \times 4 = 399$

The 100th term is 399.

Example 6: Compute $1 + 2 + 3 + \cdots + 200$.

Solution:

$$\begin{aligned}\text{Sum of the sequence} &= (1 + 200) \times 200 \div 2 \\ &= 201 \times 100 \\ &= 20{,}100\end{aligned}$$

The sum of the sequence is 20,100.

978-1-62399-075-6
Singapore Math Challenge

1. Compute $1 + 2 + 3 + \cdots + 98 + 99 + 100$.

2. Compute $1 + 3 + 5 + 7 + \cdots + 97 + 99$.

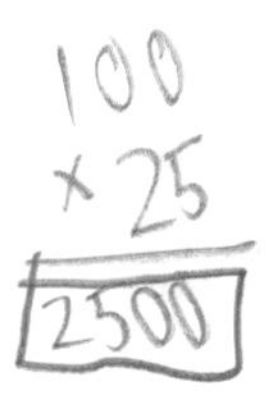

978-1-62399-075-6
Singapore Math Challenge

3. Compute $1 + 2 + 3 + 4 + \cdots + 48 + 49 + 50$.

51
×25
255
1020
1275

4. Compute $1 + 2 + 3 + \cdots + 99 + 100 + 99 + 98 + \cdots + 3 + 2 + 1$.

5. Compute 1 + 2 + 3 + ⋯ + 1,997 + 1,998 + 1,999.

1999000

6. In the number sequence, 4, 7, 10, ⋯ , 295, 298, which term is number 298?

7. Find the value of 7 + 15 + 23 + ⋯ + 767 + 775 + 783.

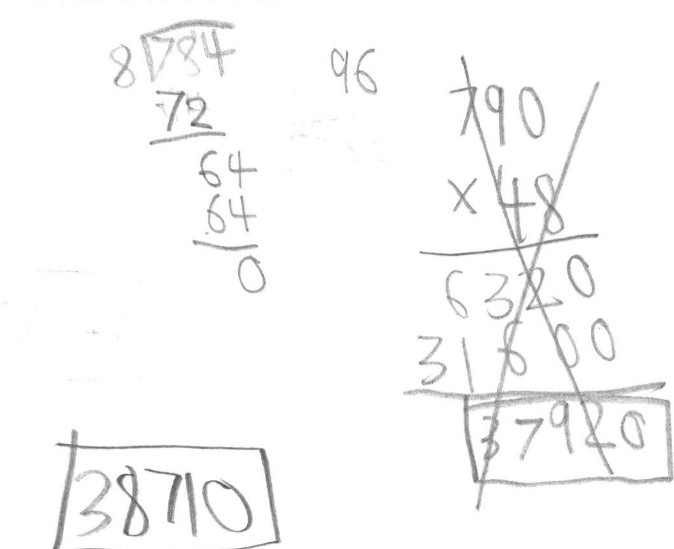

8. Each book in a series of 7 books was published once every 3 years. The fourth book was published in 1996. List the years that the rest of the books in that series were published.

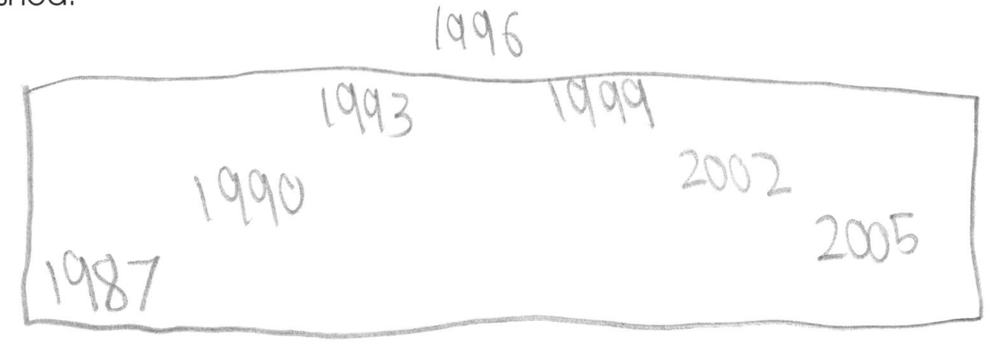

978-1-62399-075-6
Singapore Math Challenge

9. List the 8 numbers between 4 and 40 in a sequence of 10 numbers with a common difference.

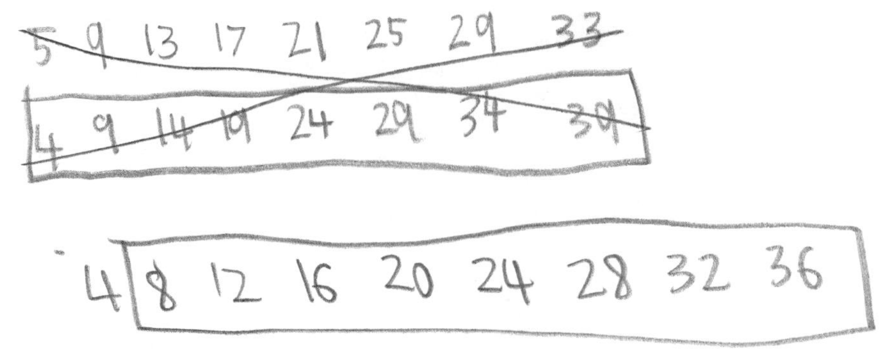

10. The sum of the sixth and seventh terms in a sequence of 12 numbers with a common difference is 15. What is the sum of the number sequence?

1 2 3 4 5 6 7 8 9 10

2 3 4 5 6 7 8 9 10 11 12 13

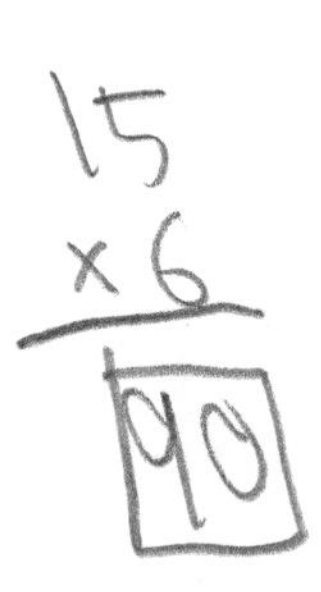

11. Place 3 numbers between 12 and 60 to make a sequence of 5 numbers with a common difference.

16 32 48 64 80

12. 20 school teams took part in the West Valley Table Tennis Tournament. Each team was to play exactly 1 match with every other team. How many matches were played altogether?

19
× 10
190

13. There are 30 rows of seats in the North Wing of a stadium. Each row has 2 seats more than the row in front. The last row has 132 seats. How many seats does the first row have? How many seats are there altogether in the North Wing of the stadium?

74

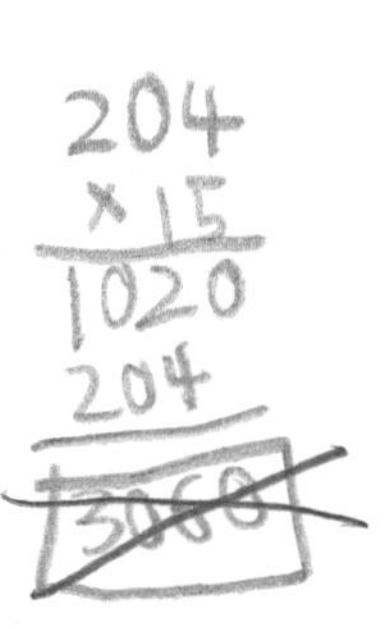

3090

14. Find the sum of all odd numbers from 1 to 100 that are not divisible by 11.

1 3 5 7 9
13 15 17 19 21
23 25 27 29 31
35 37 39 41 43
45 47 49 51 53
57 59 61 63 65
67 69 71 73 75
79 81 83 85 87
89 91 93 95 97

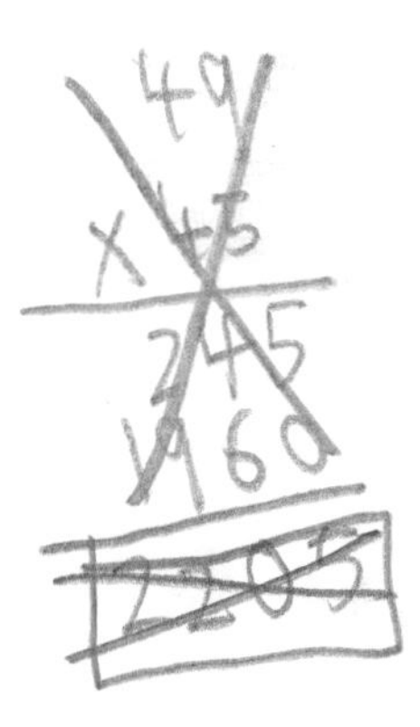

978-1-62399-075-6
Singapore Math Challenge

Prime Numbers

A prime number is a number that is only divisible by itself and the number 1. The common prime numbers are 2, 3, 5, 7, ...

Example 1: List all the numbers from 1 to 30 and circle all the prime numbers.

Solution:

1	(2)	(3)	4	(5)	6	(7)	8	9	10
(11)	12	(13)	14	15	16	(17)	18	(19)	20
21	22	(23)	24	25	26	27	28	(29)	30

978-1-62399-075-6
Singapore Math Challenge

Example 2: The sum of two prime numbers is 25. Find the product of the two prime numbers.

Solution:

$2 + 23 = 25$ (the two prime numbers are 2 and 23)
$2 \times 23 = 46$

The product of the two prime numbers is 46.

Example 3: The product of two prime numbers is 51. What is the sum of the two prime numbers? What is the difference of the two prime numbers?

Solution:

$17 \times 3 = 51$
$17 + 3 = 20$
The sum of the two prime numbers is 20.

$17 - 3 = 14$
The difference of the two prime numbers is 14.

978-1-62399-075-6
Singapore Math Challenge

Example 4: Prime factorization is the process whereby a number is expressed as the product of two or more prime numbers. Perform the prime factorization of the following.

(a)

180 → (2), 90 → (2), 45 → (5), 9 → (3), (3)

180 = 2 × 2 × 3 × 3 × 5

(b)

1,386 → (2), 693 → (3), 231 → (3), 77 → (7), (11)

1,386 = 2 × 3 × 3 × 7 × 11

(c)

1,260 → (2), 630 → (2), 315 → (5), 63 → (7), 9 → (3), (3)

1,260 = 2 × 2 × 3 × 3 × 5 × 7

(d)

2,574 → (2), 1,287 → (3), 429 → (3), 143 → (11), (13)

2,574 = 2 × 3 × 3 × 11 × 13

978-1-62399-075-6
Singapore Math Challenge

Example 5: The area of a rectangle is 165 cm². Find the possible values of the length and width of the rectangle.

Solution:

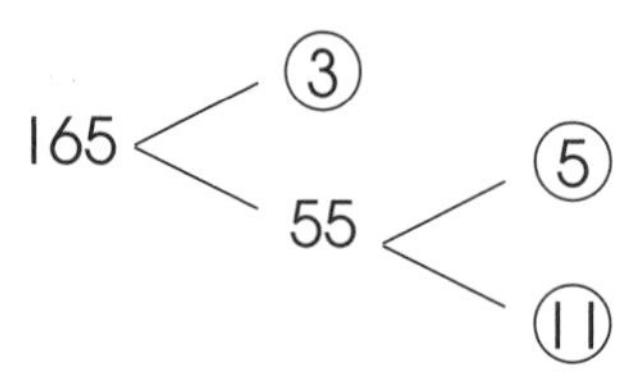

$165 = 3 \times 5 \times 11$

$1 \times 165 = 165$
$3 \times 55 = 165$
$5 \times 33 = 165$
$11 \times 15 = 165$

The possible values of the length and width of the rectangle are 1 and 165, 3 and 55, 5 and 33, and 11 and 15.

978-1-62399-075-6
Singapore Math Challenge

1. Circle all the prime numbers between 30 and 60 from the numbers below.

31	32	33	34	35	36	37	38	39	40
41	42	43	44	45	46	47	48	49	50
51	52	53	54	55	56	57	58	59	60

978-1-62399-075-6
Singapore Math Challenge

Name ______________________ Date __________

2. The sum of two prime numbers is 39. Find the product of the two prime numbers.

3. List all the 1-digit, 2-digit and 3-digit numbers using the numbers 1, 2 and 3. Each digit is to be used only once in each number. What are the prime numbers in this list?

1 2 3 12 13 21 23 31 32

123 132 213 231 312 321

2 3 13 23 31

978-1-62399-075-6
Singapore Math Challenge

4. The product of two prime numbers is 65. What is the sum of the two prime numbers? What is the difference of the two prime numbers?

5. The sum of three prime numbers is 30. There is more than one answer. Which group of prime numbers gives the smallest product?

978-1-62399-075-6

6. List the multiples of 6 that are greater than 60 but less than 100. Write down the numbers that come right before and after these multiples. Write down your observations, too.

59 60 61
65 66 67
71 72 73
77 78 79
83 84 85
89 90 91
95 96 97

They are either a prime number or the product of two prime numbers.

7. A is a prime number. A + 6, A + 8, A + 12, A + 14 are also prime numbers. What is A?

8. The sum of two prime numbers is 50. Find the biggest possible product of the two prime numbers.

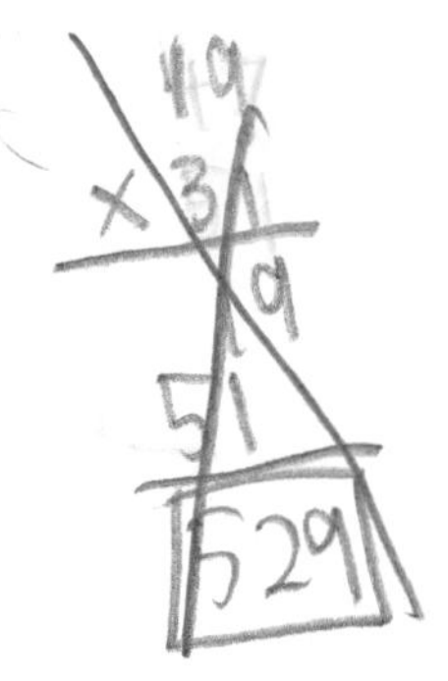

978-1-62399-075-6
Singapore Math Challenge

9. Write down 3 prime numbers that have a sum of 27. What is the biggest possible product of the 3 prime numbers?

5 11 11 121

429

978-1-62399-075-6
Singapore Math Challenge

10. Are these numbers prime numbers?

(a) 91

(b) 101

(c) 119

(d) 123

No

(e) 127

(f) 133

Name ______________________ Date ____________

11. Prime factorization is the process whereby a number is written as the product of two or more prime numbers.

$18 = 2 \times 3 \times 3$

Perform the prime factorization of the following numbers.

(a) 210

2×3×5×7

(b) 330 2×3×5×11

(c) 286

2×11×13

(d) 385

5×7×11

(e) 221

13×17

(f) 418

2×

2×13×17

(g) 1,105

5×13×17

(h) 1,309

7×11×17

978-1-62399-075-6
Singapore Math Challenge

12. To test if a number is a prime number, we must
 (a) find a number, k, such that k^2 > the number we are testing;
 (b) divide the number by all the prime numbers smaller than k.

Example: To test if a number, 529, is a prime number, we must find a number, k, such that its square is greater than 529.

$24 \times 24 = 576$ (> 529)

Divide 529 by all the prime numbers smaller than 24.

Prime numbers smaller than 24 = 2, 3, 5, 7, 11, 17, 19, 23

$529 \div 23 = 23$

529 is not a prime number since it can be divided by numbers other than 1 and itself.

978-1-62399-075-6

Are the following numbers prime numbers?

(a) 137

Yes

(b) 271

Yes

(c) 337

Yes

(d) 437

No

(e) 507

No

(f) 741

No

978-1-62399-075-6
Singapore Math Challenge

13. Perform the prime factorization of 2,006. What is the sum of all its prime factors?

78

14. Perform the prime factorization of 1,992. What is the sum of all its prime factors?

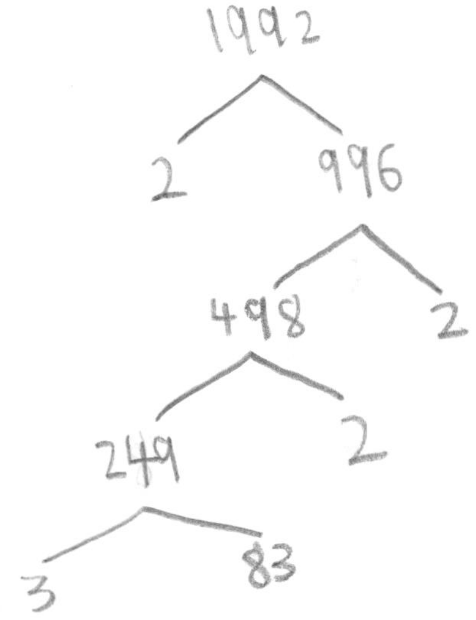

9 + 83 = 92

15. The length, width and height of the rectangular prism shown below are prime numbers. Given that A + B = 220 cm^2, find the volume of the rectangular prism. (Note that the rectangular prism below is not drawn to scale.)

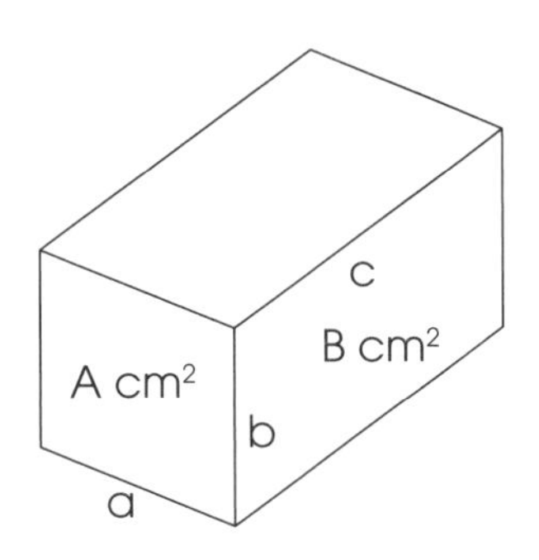

978-1-62399-075-6
Singapore Math Challenge

 Name ______________________ Date ____________

16. The product of 1,540 and m is a square number.
Find the smallest possible value of m.

1540
3080
4620
6160
7700

17. A number and another number that read the same when reversed are a palindrome pair. A good example is 243 and 342. The product of a palindrome pair is 101,088. Find the sum of the palindrome pair.

300
300

978-1-62399-075-6

 Name ______________________ Date __________

18. How many rectangles of different sizes can be formed from 36 identical rectangles?

1 36
2 18
3 12
4 9
6 6

19. In 780 × a = 1,716 × b, find the smallest values of a and b.

1	780	1716	1
			2
10	7800	3432	4
11	8580	6864	
		8580	5

20. Different whole numbers are written on each face of a cube. The sum of two whole numbers on opposite faces equals each of the 2 other sums of the whole numbers on opposite faces. The face opposite 18 is a prime number, a. The face opposite 14 is another prime number, b. Lastly, the prime number, c, is opposite a whole number, 35.
What is the value of a + b + c?

19 23 2

978-1-62399-075-6
Singapore Math Challenge

21. In how many ways is 37 a sum of 3 or more prime numbers?

11 + 13 + 13

9 + 9 + 19

978-1-62399-075-6

Divisibility

It is common sense to us that all numbers are divisible by 1.
It follows that all even numbers are divisible by 2.

What rules govern divisibility by other numbers, say, by 3, 7 or 11?
This will be of interest in this chapter.

(A) Divisibility by 3 and by 9

If a number is divisible by 3 and by 9, the sum of all its digits can be divided by 3 and by 9 respectively.

Example 1: Test the following numbers for divisibility by 3 and by 9.

(a) 312
$3 + 1 + 2 = 6$
312 is divisible by 3
but not by 9.

(b) 443
$4 + 4 + 3 = 11$
443 is not divisible
by 3 or by 9.

(c) 567
$5 + 6 + 7 = 18$
576 is divisible by 3
and by 9.

(c) 818
$8 + 1 + 8 = 17$
818 is not divisible
by 3 or by 9.

978-1-62399-075-6
Singapore Math Challenge

(B) Divisibility by 4 and by 25

If the last two digits of a number can be divided by 4, the number is divisible by 4. Divisibility by 25 is governed by the same rule.

Example 2: Test the following numbers for divisibility by 4.

(a) 1,016

1,016 is divisible by 4 since its last 2 digits, 16, can be divided by 4.

(b) 3,234

3,234 is not divisible by 4 since 34 cannot be divided by 4.

(c) 2,348

2,348 is divisible by 4 since 48 can be divided by 4.

(d) 1,558

1,558 is not divisible by 4 since 58 cannot be divided by 4.

978-1-62399-075-6
Singapore Math Challenge

Example 3: Test the following numbers for their divisibility by 25.

(a) 1,025

1,025 is divisible by 25 as its last 2 digits, 25, can be divided by 25.

(b) 2,235

2,235 is not divisible by 25 as 35 cannot be divided by 25.

(c) 3,175

3,175 is divisible by 25 as 75 can be divided by 25.

(d) 4,445

4,445 is not divisible by 25 as 45 cannot be divided by 25.

978-1-62399-075-6
Singapore Math Challenge

(C) Divisibility by 8 and by 125

If the last three digits of a number are divisible by 8, the number is divisible by 8. The same goes for divisibility by 125.

Example 4: Test the following numbers for divisibility by 8 and by 125.

(a) 13,125

13,125 is not divisible by 8.
It is divisible by 125 as its last 3 digits are 125.

(b) 132,000

132,000 is divisible by 8 and by 125 as 000 is divisible by both numbers.

(c) 52,450

52,450 is not divisible by either number as 450 is not divisible by 8 or by 125.

(d) 12,400

12,400 is divisible by 8 as 450 is divisible by 8.
It is not divisible by 125.

978-1-62399-075-6
Singapore Math Challenge

(D) Divisibility by 7 and by 13

> If the difference of the last three digits of a number and all its preceding digits can be divided by 7 or by 13, the number is divisible by 7 or by 13.

Example 5: Are the following numbers divisible by 7 or by 13?

(a) 2,093

93 – 2 = 91
91 can be divided by 7 and by 13. Therefore, 2,093 is divisible by 7 and by 13.

(b) 4,095

95 – 4 = 91
4,095 is divisible by 7 and by 13.

(c) 16,042

42 – 16 = 26
16,042 is divisible by 13 as 26 can be divided by 13.
It is not divisible by 7 as 26 is not a multiple of 7.

(d) 54,864

864 – 54 = 810
54,864 is not divisible by 7 or by 13 as 810 cannot be divided by 7 or by 13.

978-1-62399-075-6
Singapore Math Challenge

(E) Divisibility by 11

If the difference of the sum of the digits in the even place values and the sum of the digits in the odd place values is 0 or a multiple of 11, the number is divisible by 11.

Example 6: Check the following numbers for divisibility by 11.

(a) 135,795

$(3 + 7 + 5) - (1 + 5 + 9) = 15 - 15 = 0$
135,795 is divisible by 11 since the difference is 0.

(b) 258,016

$(5 + 0 + 6) - (2 + 8 + 1) = 11 - 11 = 0$
258,016 is divisible by 11 since the difference is 0.

(c) 123,456

$(2 + 4 + 6) - (1 + 3 + 5) = 12 - 9 = 3$
123,456 is not divisible by 11 since the difference is neither 0 nor 11.

(d) 234,765

$(3 + 7 + 5) - (2 + 4 + 6) = 15 - 12 = 3$
234,765 is not divisible by 11 since the difference is neither 0 nor 11.

978-1-62399-075-6
Singapore Math Challenge

Example 7: If 45,67m is divisible by 3, find the possible values of m.

Solution:

4 + 5 + 6 + 7 = 22
22 + 2 = 24
22 + 5 = 27
22 + 8 = 30

The possible values of m are 2, 5 and 8.

Example 8: A 6-digit number begins with the digit 7. The number is divisible by 9. All six digits of the number are different. Find the smallest possible value of this number.

Solution:

We have 7 □ □ □ □ □.
To make the 6-digit number the smallest, we choose 0, 1, 2 and 3. The number then becomes

7 0 1 2 3 □
7 + 0 + 1 + 2 + 3 = 13
13 + 5 = 18 is divisible by 9

The smallest possible value of this number is 701,235.

978-1-62399-075-6
Singapore Math Challenge

Example 9: Find the values represented by □ in the 6-digit number, 458,□□□, such that this number is the smallest and divisible by 3, 4 and 5.

Solution:

The last 2 digits must be 00 in order to be divisible by 4 and by 5.

We have 458,□ 00.

4 + 5 + 8 = 17
17 + □ = 18 (to be divisible by 3)
□ = 18 − 17 = 1

The values represented by □ are 1, 0 and 0 respectively.

978-1-62399-075-6

1. Check the following numbers for divisibility by 3 and by 9.

(a) 2,367

3 yes

9 yes

(b) 10,002

3 yes

9 no

(c) 18,135

3 yes

9 yes

(d) 10,032

3 yes

9 no

978-1-62399-075-6
Singapore Math Challenge

2. If a number is given as 1,234, its palindromic number is 4,321. Is 5,154 divisible by 3? How about its palindromic number, 4,515? Why?

Yes.
Yes. If the sum of the digits is divisible by 3, then yes.

3. If a number is not divisible by 10, can it be divided by 5?

Yes.

4. If a number is not divisible by 5, can it be divided by 10?

978-1-62399-075-6
Singapore Math Challenge

5. Test the following numbers for divisibility by 7 and by 13.

(a) 15,041

7 no
13 yes

(b) 397,523

126

7 yes
13 no

(c) 415,597

182

7 yes
13 yes

(d) 417,508

91

7 yes
13 yes

978-1-62399-075-6
Singapore Math Challenge

6. A palindromic number is a number that reads the same forward and backward. 4,567,654 is a palindromic number. Check 4,567,654 for divisibility by 9 and by 11.

11 yes 9 no

```
    50951
9 ) 4567654
    45
     67
     63
      46
      45
       15
        9
       64
```


978-1-62399-075-6
Singapore Math Challenge

7. Check the following palindromic numbers for divisibility by 11. Are you able to draw any conclusion?

(a) 386,683

33
55
11
55
33
Yes

(b) 156,651

Yes

(c) 23,788,732

22
11
66
22
66
11
22
Yes

(d) 12,344,321

11
11
22
22
22
11
11
Yes

978-1-62399-075-6
Singapore Math Challenge

8. Test 3,466,645 for divisibility by 13.

9. Write down any 3-digit number. Repeat the 3 digits to make it a 6-digit number. Divide the 6-digit number by 13. Divide again by 11. Lastly, divide the quotient from the second division by 7. What do you get? Why?

9471
13) 123123
117
61
52
92
91
13
13
0

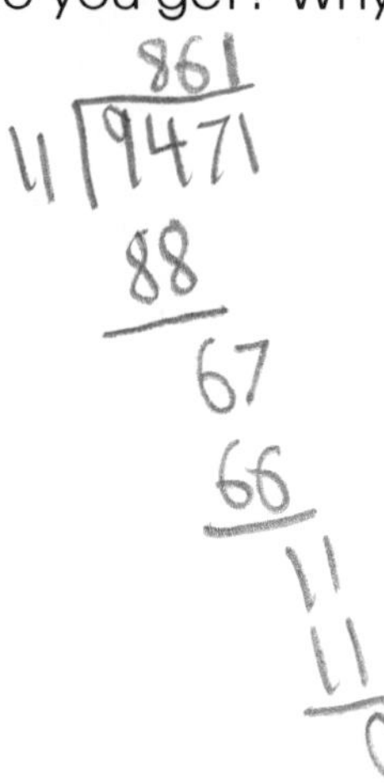

123
7) 861
7
16
14
21
21
0

10. Check the following numbers for divisibility by 3 and by 9.

(a) 1,278

3 yes
9 yes

(b) 4,632

3 yes
9 no

(c) 54,684

3 yes
9 yes

(d) 119,375

3 no
9 no

978-1-62399-075-6
Singapore Math Challenge

11. Check the following numbers for divisibility by 4, 8, 25 and 125.

(a) 37,625

4 no
8 no
25 yes
125 yes

(b) 93,648

4 yes
8 yes
25 no
125 no

(c) 87,615

4 no
8 no
25 no
125 no

(d) 1,548,672

4 yes
8 yes
25 no
125 no

978-1-62399-075-6
Singapore Math Challenge

12. Check 517,699 for divisibility by 7 and by 13.

182

7 yes
13 yes

13. If 50,15m is divisible by 3, find the possible values of m.

978-1-62399-075-6
Singapore Math Challenge

14. Find the digits represented by a and b in a78,89b and the possible values of the number so that it is divisible by 15.

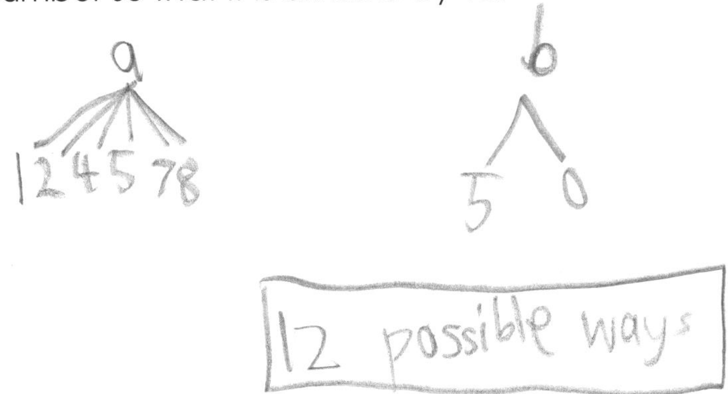

15. Find the possible values of a in 3,333,33a,888,888 so that the number is divisible by 7.

16. A 7-digit number, 2,006,□□□, is divisible by 3, by 4 and by 25. Find the missing digits and the possible values of this number.

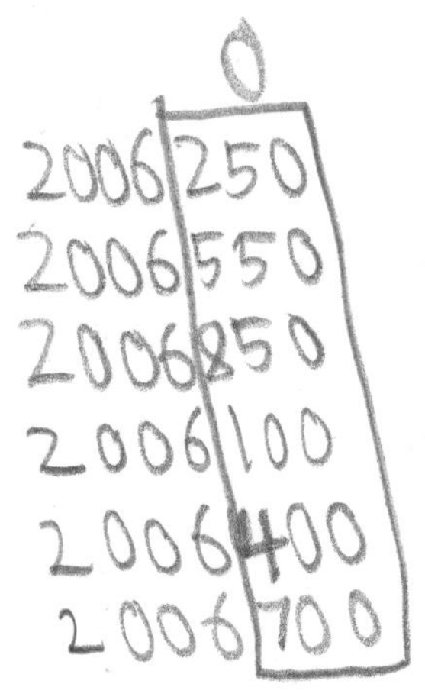

17. What is the largest possible value of □89,49□ if it is divisible by 11?

978-1-62399-075-6
Singapore Math Challenge

18. Find the possible values of ☐ in the number 25,☐ 4 ☐ if it is divisible by 3 and by 5.

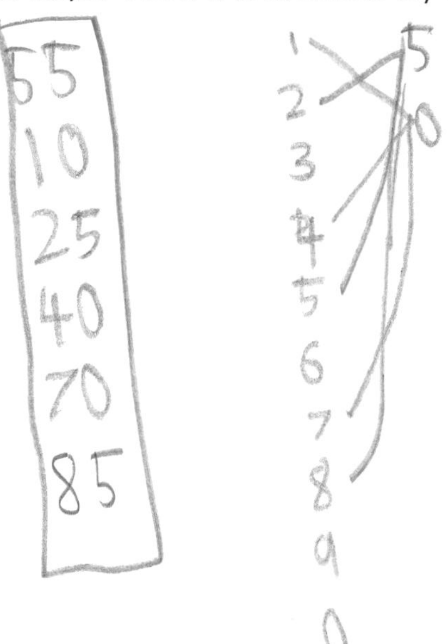

19. How many whole numbers between 1 and 100 are not divisible by 3 or by 11?

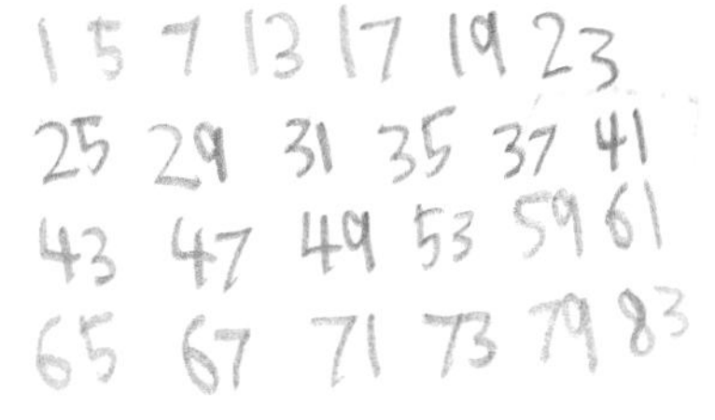

978-1-62399-075-6
Singapore Math Challenge

20. Test 35,112 for divisibility by 7, by 11 and by 13.

7 yes

11 yes

13 no

21. Find the possible values of □ and the possible values of the number 5□,34□ so that it is divisible by 5 and by 9.

978-1-62399-075-6
Singapore Math Challenge

22. Find the smallest possible value of the number 368,□□□ so that it is divisible by 3, 4 and 25.

100
400
700

100

23. A 6-digit number begins with the digit 8. The number is divisible by 9. All digits of the number are different. What is the smallest possible value of this number?

978-1-62399-075-6
Singapore Math Challenge

Logic

Logic is a branch of mathematics that relies more on strong reasoning skills rather than on computational capability.

The techniques often used are listed below.

(A) Assume something to be true until it is proven otherwise.

(B) Make a systematic list so as to scrutinize the given information.

(C) Make a table or a few tables.
Sometimes, we can even draw them out!

978-1-62399-075-6

Example 1: Four spectators were commenting on the outcome of a 100-m race.

David : A came in second and B came in third.
Sophia : C was in fourth place and B was in second place.
Shane : D finished second and C finished third.
Jodie : D was in first place and B was in third place.

Only one remark in each comment is true. In what position was C?

Solution:

If David was right about A, B was neither in second nor third place. It follows that C would be in both the third place and fourth place. So, A could not have come in second.

We can make a table to check all the information. Begin with B in third place.

	A	B	C	D
First	✓			
Second				✓
Third		✓		
Fourth			✓	

C was in the fourth position.

978-1-62399-075-6
Singapore Math Challenge

Example 2: A policeman detained four suspects for a theft case.

A: Hey, I didn't do it!

B: A did it.

C: Come on, I was not even there when the crime took place.

D: B did it.

Only one suspect told the truth. Who was the thief?

Solution:

If A did it, both B and C would have told the truth.
So, A is not the thief.

If B did it, A, C and D would have told the truth.

If C did it, A would have told the truth. B, C and D had lied.

C was the thief.

978-1-62399-075-6

Example 3: Some years ago, there were 5 Wednesdays and 4 Tuesdays in the month of March. On which day of the week was August 1st in that year?

Solution:

31 ÷ 7 = 4 R 3

There were 4 sets of four days of the week in the month of March. There were 5 sets of 3 days in the month of March.

Sun.	Mon.	Tue.	Wed.	Thur.	Fri.	Sat.
			1	2	3	4
5	6	7	R_1	R_2	R_3	R_4
R_5	R_6	R_0				

31 + 30 + 31 + 30 + 31 + 1 = 154

From March 1st to August 1st, there were 154 days.

154 ÷ 7 = 22 R 0

August 1st was a Tuesday in that year.

978-1-62399-075-6
Singapore Math Challenge

1. Stanley wrote a 4-digit number on a piece of paper and challenged Darrell to guess it. All the digits were different.

Darrell : **Is it 4,607?**
Stanley : **Two of the numbers are correct but they are positioned wrongly.**
Darrell : **Could it be 1,385?**
Stanley : **My answer is the same as before.**
Darrell: **How about 2,879?**
Stanley : **Wow, two of the numbers are correct and in the right places as well.**
Darrell : **5,461?**
Stanley : **None of the digits is correct.**

What was the number?

978-1-62399-075-6
Singapore Math Challenge

2. A box contains blue marbles. Another two boxes contain only white marbles.
Label on Box A : white marbles
Label on Box B : blue marbles
Label on Box C : Box B contains blue marbles
Which box contains blue marbles if two of the above labels are mixed up?

Box B

978-1-62399-075-6

3. Andrew, Jolene and Tommy each draw 3 cards from 9 cards numbered 1, 2, 3, ..., 9.
Andrew : The product of all my numbers is 48.
Jolene : The sum of all my numbers is 16.
Tommy : The product of all my numbers is 63.
What is the largest number among Jolene's cards?

1 2 3 4 5 6 7 8 9

Andrew: 2, 4, 6
Jolene: 3, 5, 8
Tommy: 1, 7, 9

4. What is the 5th number in the 15th row of the number triangle shown below?

1

2 3

4 5 6

7 8 9 10

11 12 13 14 15

... ...

... ...

5. Three girls are talking about their ages.

Ashley : **I am 12 years old, 3 years Stella's junior but 1 year older than Melanie.**

Stella : **I am not the youngest. Melanie and I are 4 years apart. Ashley is 11 years old.**

Melanie : **I am younger than Ashley. She is 10 years old. Stella is 2 years her senior.**

One of the above three statements made by each girl is incorrect. Help them unscramble this age puzzle.

	Ashley	Stella	Melanie
Ashley	12	15	11
Stella	11	14	10
Melanie	10	12	9

978-1-62399-075-6
Singapore Math Challenge

6. A meteorological report shows the following records of a certain number of days.
It rained 10 times, either in the morning or in the afternoon.
There were 8 dry afternoons.
There were 14 dry mornings.
Each wet afternoon was preceded by a dry morning.
How many days did the meteorologist record?

978-1-62399-075-6
Singapore Math Challenge

7. Among Andy, Kevin and Matthew, one of them is a teacher. The other two are a doctor and a police officer.
Matthew is older than the police officer.
Andy and the doctor are not the same age.
The doctor is younger than Kevin.
Who is the teacher?

Matthew < police
Andy < doctor < Kevin

~~Andy~~ Matthew = doctor

978-1-62399-075-6
Singapore Math Challenge

8. Teddy : Both Leon and Peter lied.
Leon : One of them (Teddy or Peter) was lying.
Peter : One of them (Teddy or Leon) told the truth.
Who lied? Who told the truth?

Teddy lied
Leon and Peter told the truth

978-1-62399-075-6
Singapore Math Challenge

9. One of the three ladies, Amanda, Beatrice and Jodie, comes from Town A. The other two ladies come from Town B and Town C.
Jodie is older than the lady from Town B.
Amanda and the lady from Town C are not the same age.
The lady from Town C is younger than Beatrice.
Who comes from Town A?

Jodie > B
C < Beatrice

Beatrice

978-1-62399-075-6
Singapore Math Challenge

10. The target board for a dart game with different scores in each ring is shown below.

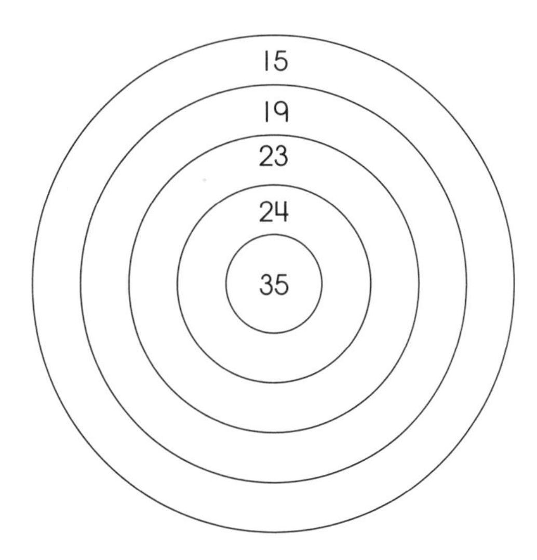

Each round of practice comes with 6 darts.
How does Dave manage to have a score of 130?

23
23
23
23
23
15

$$23 \times 5 = 115$$

11. A football flew through the glass window of the teacher's room and shattered it into pieces. Four probable culprits were called to the principal for investigation.

Colin : Jason did it!
Jason : David did it!
Melvin : Not me!
David : Jason did it! His words cannot be trusted.

Only one student told the truth.
Who was the culprit?

978-1-62399-075-6
Singapore Math Challenge

12. Alicia, Beatrice, Charles, David, Elaine, Florence, Graham and Herman are four couples.
Elaine attended David's wedding as a guest.
Alicia's husband is a cousin of Herman.
When Herman went overseas with his spouse, Beatrice, Charles and Elaine each represented their own spouses to see the couple off at the airport.
Help to match the four couples.

Florence — Herman
Beatrice — David
Elaine — Graham
Alicia — Charles

978-1-62399-075-6
Singapore Math Challenge

13. Four tourists, A, B, C and D, check into an 18-story hotel.
The countries of their origin are China, Germany, Mexico and Egypt.
The floor number where A is staying is 4 times that of the Mexican's.
The German stays 4 floors higher than B but lower than the Egyptian.
The Egyptian stays 6 floors lower than A.
All the floor numbers of their hotel rooms are even.
Match A, B, C and D to their countries of origin and the floor numbers of their hotel rooms.

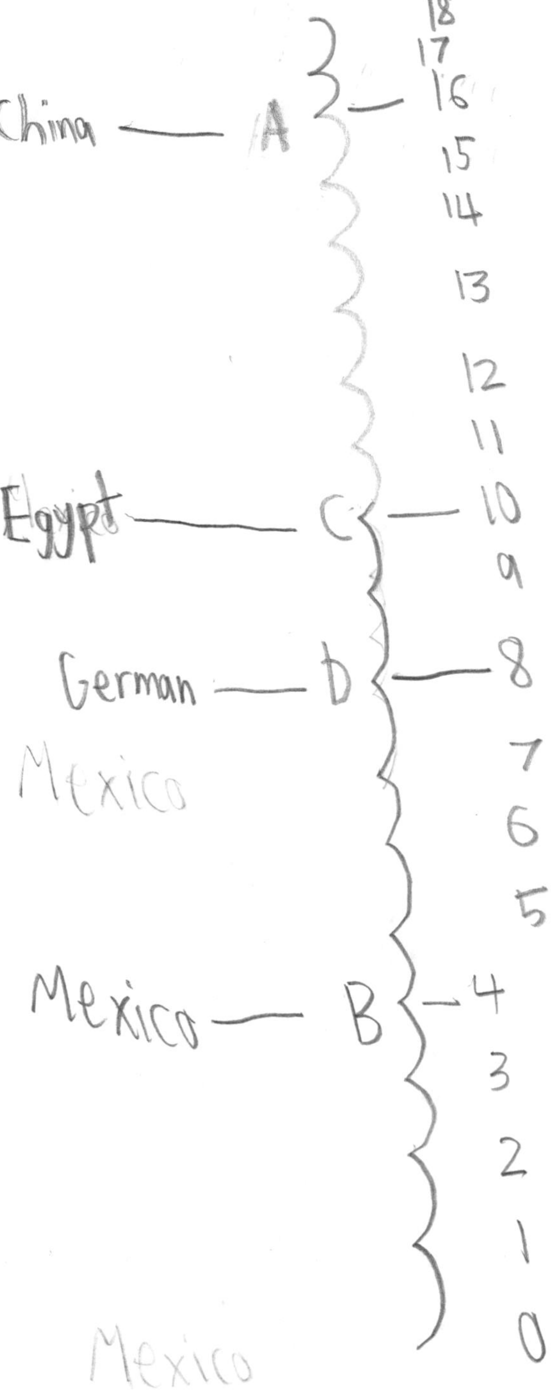

14. Melissa, Amy and Tony come from different schools, namely Greenville, Bloomsberry and Windschill Elementary Schools. Each of them likes one of the following sports: swimming, basketball or volleyball.
Melissa does not go to Greenville.
Amy does not go to Bloomsberry.
The student who likes volleyball does not attend Windschill.
The student who likes swimming is from Greenville.
Match the three students to their sports and schools.

Melissa – Bloomsberry, Windschill
Amy – Greenville, Windschill

Basketball – Amy – Windschill
Swimming – Tony – Greenville
Volleyball – Melissa – Bloomsberry

Write Simple Equations

To think algebraically is to write a simple equation or a group of equations. It can help solve a wide range of questions involving:

(i) **1 equation with 1 unknown**, like in Example 3 and practice questions 1 and 2.

(ii) **1 equation with 2 unknowns**. The technique to solve this type of problem is shown in Example 4 and practice questions 5, 7 and 8.

(iii) **2 equations with 2 unknowns**. Students may already be familiar with these types of problems.

(iv) **2 equations with 3 unknowns**. The trick to this type of question is to reduce it to 2 equations with 2 unknowns by comparison and elimination, so it becomes manageable. Example 5 and practice questions 13 and 14 belong to this class.

(v) A **group of equations**. Students should look for ways to reduce them to one equation.

In algebra, the multiplication symbol "×" is often omitted, just in case it is mixed up with "x."

978-1-62399-075-6
Singapore Math Challenge

Example 1: 2 peaches and 12 apples cost $14.60.
6 peaches and 4 apples cost $18.20.
How much is an apple?
How much is a peach?

Solution:

Let *p* and *a* be peach and apple respectively.

$2p + 12a \rightarrow \$14.60$
$6p + 4a \rightarrow \$18.20$
$6p + 36a \rightarrow 3 \times \$14.60 = \$43.80$
$32a \rightarrow \$43.80 - \$18.20 = \$25.60$
$a \rightarrow \$25.60 \div 32 = \$0.80$
$2p \rightarrow \$14.60 - 12 \times \$0.80 = \$5$
$2p \rightarrow \$5$
$p \rightarrow \$5 \div 2 = \$2.50$

An apple is $0.80. A peach is $2.50.

978-1-62399-075-6
Singapore Math Challenge

Example 2: There are 160 white and blue balls, 180 blue and yellow balls, and 170 white and yellow balls. Find the number of balls for each color.

Solution:

Let w, b and y be white, blue and yellow balls respectively.

$$
\begin{aligned}
w + b &\rightarrow 160 \\
b + y &\rightarrow 180 \\
w + y &\rightarrow 170 \\
2w + 2b + 2y &\rightarrow 160 + 180 + 170 = 510 \\
w + b + y &\rightarrow 510 \div 2 = 255 \\
y &\rightarrow 255 - 160 = 95 \\
w &\rightarrow 255 - 180 = 75 \\
b &\rightarrow 255 - 170 = 85
\end{aligned}
$$

There are 95 yellow balls, 75 white balls and 85 blue balls.

978-1-62399-075-6

Example 3: The sum of Michelle's, her mother's and her grandmother's ages is 100. Her grandmother is twice as old as her mother. Her mother is 28 years older than Michelle. How old is her grandmother?

Solution:

Let Michelle's age be m.

$$
\begin{aligned}
m + m + 28 + 2(m + 28) &= 100 \\
2m + 28 + 2m + 56 &= 100 \\
4m + 84 &= 100 \\
4m &= 100 - 84 = 16 \\
m &= 16 \div 4 = 4 \\
2(m + 28) &= 2(4 + 28) \\
&= 64
\end{aligned}
$$

Her grandmother is 64 years old.

978-1-62399-075-6
Singapore Math Challenge

Example 4: The sum of two numbers is 189.
One number is a multiple of 13.
The other number is a multiple of 17.
Find the two numbers.

Solution:

Let the first number be m and the second number be n.

$$13 \times m + 17 \times n = 189$$
$$13m = 189 - 17n$$
$$m = \frac{189 - 17n}{13}$$

$189 - 17n$ is a multiple of 13.

When $n = 5$,

$$189 - 17 \times 5 = 104$$
$$104 \div 13 = 8$$

These two numbers are 85 and 104.

978-1-62399-075-6
Singapore Math Challenge

Example 5: A school librarian bought 30 books for a total of \$130. A storybook cost \$4, while a science book and a math book cost \$6 and \$5 respectively. How many books in each category did she buy?

Solution:

Let a, b and c represent the types of books. We have

$a + b + c = 30$ .... (1)

The cost of a, b and c are \$4, \$6 and \$5 respectively.

$4a + 6b + 5c = 130$ .... (2)

We try to eliminate one unknown.

$(1) \times 4$

$4a + 4b + 4c = 120$ .... (3)

(2) - (3)

$2b + c = 10$

One possible answer:

$b = 3$, $c = 4$, then $a = 23$

Another possible answer:

$b = 2$, $c = 6$, then $a = 22$

1. Find five consecutive numbers whose sum is 465.

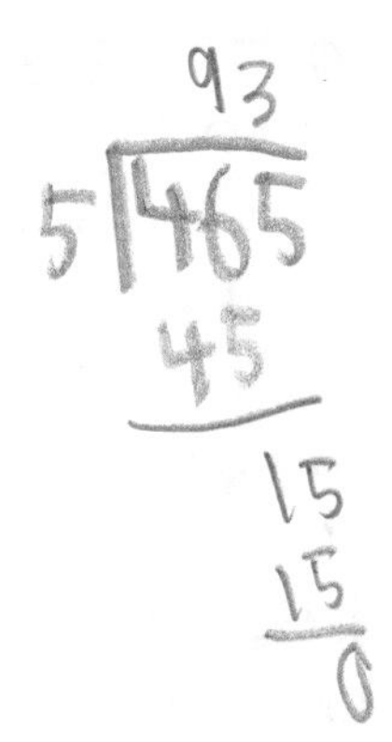

2. A teacher has a bag of candy. If she gives every student in her class 4 pieces of candy, she is left with 48 pieces of candy. If she gives every student 6 pieces of candy, she needs another 8 pieces of candy. How many students does she give the sweets to?

48 + 8 = 56

978-1-62399-075-6
Singapore Math Challenge

3. On March 1st some years ago, one US dollar could be exchanged for 1.45 Singapore dollars. On the same day, 1,000 Thai Baht could buy 50 Singapore dollars. How many US dollars could 29,000 Thai Baht buy on that day?

1us = 1.45s

20t = 1s

29t = 1.45s

978-1-62399-075-6
Singapore Math Challenge

4. 4 footballs and 4 volleyballs cost $240.
3 footballs and 5 volleyballs cost $234.
What is the cost of a football?
What is the cost of a volleyball?

$4f + 4v = 240$
$3f + 5v = 234$

football = 33
Volleyball = 27

978-1-62399-075-6
Singapore Math Challenge

5. There is a total of 62 tennis balls.
A long tube can hold 5 balls.
A short tube can hold 3 balls.
How many long tubes are there?

978-1-62399-075-6
Singapore Math Challenge

6. A farmer has 145 chickens and rabbits. 410 legs are counted altogether. How many chickens does the farmer have? How many rabbits does the farmer have?

chickens	rabbits	
145	0	290
45	100	490
85	60	410

978-1-62399-075-6
Singapore Math Challenge

7. A big box can hold 12 marbles and a small box can hold 5 marbles. There are a total of 99 marbles. How many big boxes are there?

978-1-62399-075-6
Singapore Math Challenge

8. Jonathan multiplies the month of his birthday by 31. He then multiplies the day of his birthday by 12. The sum of the two products is 213. When is Jonathan's birthday?

31
62
93

10

978-1-62399-075-6
Singapore Math Challenge

 Name ______________________ Date ____________

9. Find the value of C in the following.

		A
A	C	B
B	D	D
C	E	E
31	47	64

31 + 47 = 78

78 − 64 = 14

978-1-62399-075-6
Singapore Math Challenge

10. 3 packets of french fries, 2 cheeseburgers and 1 drink cost \$10.95.
1 packet of french fries, 2 cheeseburgers and 3 drinks cost \$11.25.
Find the price of one packet of french fries, one cheeseburger and one drink.

$3f + 2c + 1d = 10.95$

$1f + 2c + 3d = 11.25$

978-1-62399-075-6
Singapore Math Challenge

 Name ____________________ Date ____________

11. ▣ + ∷ + ⊙ + ⊙ = 52
▣ + ∷ + ∷ + ⊙ = 47
▣ + ▣ + ∷ + ⊙ = 49

Find the values of ▣, ∷ and ⊙.

▣ = ∷ + 2
⊙ = ▣ + 3

∷ = 10
▣ = 12
⊙ = 15

978-1-62399-075-6
Singapore Math Challenge

12. 3 of item A, 7 of item B and 1 of item C in a toy collection cost $31.50.
4 of item A, 10 of item B and 1 of item C in the same collection cost $42.
Find the price of item A + item B + item C.

$3a + 7b + 1c = 31.5$
$4a + 10b + 1c = 42$

$a + 3b = 10.5$

$6 + 3 + 1.5$

978-1-62399-075-6
Singapore Math Challenge

13. A math competition has been held every year for the past 20 years. Each year, the competition has been based on 20 questions, 25 questions or 30 questions. A total of 515 questions have been used so far. For how many years was the competition based on 25 questions?

20	25	30	
0	20	0	500
0	17	3	515
1	15	4	
3	11	6	

978-1-62399-075-6

14. Roosters cost 5 *qian* each. (A *qian* is a copper coin used in ancient China.) Hens cost 3 *qian* each and 3 chicks cost 1 *qian*. If 100 fowls were bought for 100 *qian*, how many roosters, hens and chicks were there?

1 0 99 38
1 3 96 46
1 6 93 54
1 9 90 62
1 12 87 70
1 15 84 78
1 18 81 86
1 21 78 94
4 18 78 100

978-1-62399-075-6
Singapore Math Challenge

Remainder Problems

Many interesting problems can evolve out of the remainders in division.

First, let's familiarize ourselves with the terms in a division statement.

Given a division statement, $37 \div 5 = 7$ R 2.

37 is called the dividend.
5 is called the divisor.
7 is the quotient.
2 is the remainder.

It follows:

$$\text{Dividend} = \text{Divisor} \times \text{Quotient} + \text{Remainder}$$

978-1-62399-075-6
Singapore Math Challenge

Example 1: How many numbers, when divided by 6, have the same quotient and remainder?

Solution:

$6 \times 5 + 5 = 35$
$6 \times 4 + 4 = 28$
$6 \times 3 + 3 = 21$
$6 \times 2 + 2 = 14$
$6 \times 1 + 1 = 7$

5 numbers have the same quotient and remainder.

Example 2: Today is Friday. Which day of the week will it be 80 days later, including today?

Solution:

Sun.	Mon.	Tue.	Wed.	Thur.	Fri. Today	Sat.
R3	R4	R5	R6	R0	R1	R2

$80 \div 7 = 11 \text{ R } 3$

It will be a Sunday 80 days later.

978-1-62399-075-6
Singapore Math Challenge

Example 3: A string of beads are arranged in the following pattern: 5 blue, 4 black, 4 white, 5 blue, 4 black, 4 white, and so on. What color is the 321st bead? What about the 508th bead?

Solution:

5 + 4 + 4 = 13
321 ÷ 13 = 24 R 9
508 ÷ 13 = 39 R 1

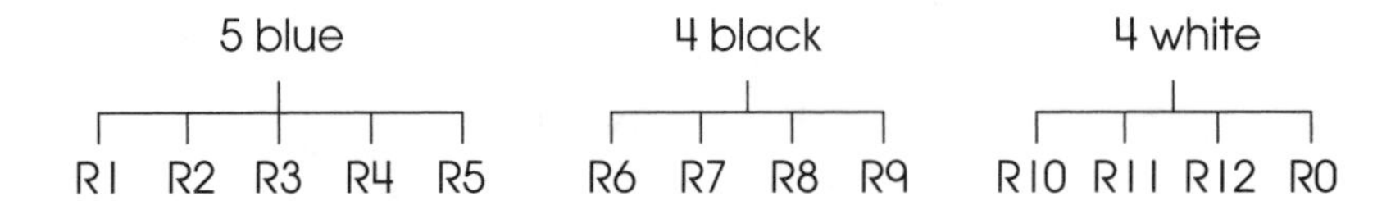

The color of the 321st bead is black.
The color of the 508th bead is blue.

Example 4: The sum of a dividend, divisor, quotient and remainder is 56. The quotient and the remainder are 4 and 6 respectively. Find the dividend and the divisor.

Solution:

56 – 4 – 6 = 46
Dividend + Divisor = 46

Since the remainder is 6, the divisor must be greater than 6.

Sum	Dividend	Divisor	
46	39	7	39 ÷ 7 = 5 R 4 ✗
46	38	8	38 ÷ 8 = 4 R 6 ✓

The dividend is 38 and the divisor is 8.

978-1-62399-075-6
Singapore Math Challenge

Example 5: A series of whole numbers are arranged as shown below.

A	1	8	9	16	...
B	2	7	10	15	...
C	3	6	11	14	...
D	4	5	12	13	...

In which row is number 500?
How many numbers are in Row C if 300 is the last number?

Solution:

The number pattern is recurring in a "U-shaped" manner.

$$500 \div 8 = 62 \text{ R } 4$$

Which row has a remainder of 4?

A	1	8	9 R 1	16 R 0
B	2	7	10 R 2	15 R 7
C	3	6	11 R 3	14 R 6
D	4	5	12 R 4	13 R 5

Number 500 is in Row D.

$$300 \div 8 = 37 \text{ R } 4$$

One block of 8 numbers has 2 columns.
37 blocks of 8 numbers has $37 \times 2 = 74$ numbers in Row C.

$$74 + 1 = 75$$

75 numbers are in Row C if 300 is the last number.

978-1-62399-075-6

Example 6: Given a number sequence, 3, 7, 5, 3, 2, 3, 7, 5, 3, 2, ...
What is the sum of the first 100 numbers?
What is the 154th number?

Solution:

The numbers are repeating after every 5 numbers.

$100 \div 5 = 20$ blocks of numbers

$3 + 7 + 5 + 3 + 2 = 20$

$20 \times 20 = 400$

The sum of the first 100 numbers is 400.

3	7	5	3	2 ...
R1	R2	R3	R4	R0

$154 \div 5 = 30$ R 4

The 154th number is 3.

978-1-62399-075-6
Singapore Math Challenge

 Name ______________________ Date ____________

1. How many numbers, when divided by 7, have the same quotient and remainder?

2. Some years ago, January 1st was a Thursday. Which day of the week was April 1st in that year? (Assume February has 28 days in that year.)

Wednesday

978-1-62399-075-6
Singapore Math Challenge

3. Today is Friday. Which day of the week will it be 90 days later, including today?

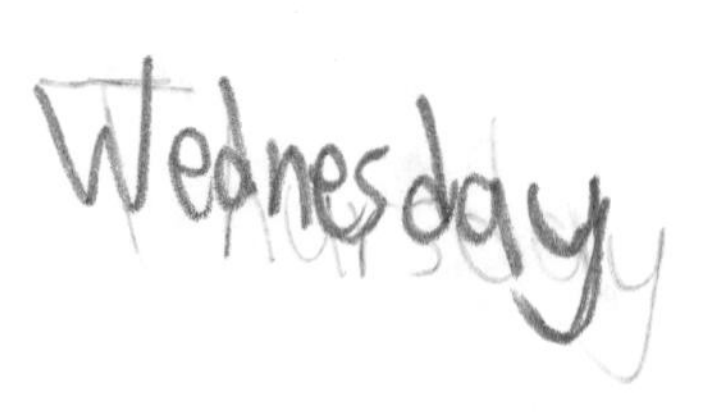

4. A 2-digit number has a remainder of 7 when it is divided by 9. It has a remainder of 5 when it is divided by 7. Find the 2-digit number.

5 7
12 16
19 25
26 34
33 43
40 52
47 61
54
61

978-1-62399-075-6
Singapore Math Challenge

5. 168 beads are strung in a sequence of 5 black, 4 blue, 3 white, 5 black, 4 blue, 3 white, and so on. What color is the 150th bead? How many blue beads are there in the first 150 beads?

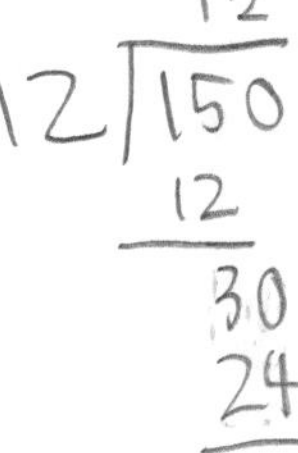

Blue

49

6. A number sequence is shown below.

3, 7, 2, 1, 5, 2, 3, 7, 2, 1, 5, 2, ...

What is the sum of the first 122 numbers?
What is the 138th number?

410

2

978-1-62399-075-6

7. Some years ago, June 1st was a Friday. Which day of the week was August 30th in that year?

8. When 120 is divided by a 2-digit number, the remainder is 12. There is no remainder when 144 is divided by this number.
Find the smallest possible value of the 2-digit number.

978-1-62399-075-6
Singapore Math Challenge

9. 1,988 rescue packages were distributed to seven regions affected by natural disasters, as shown below.

A	B	C	D	E	F	G
1	2	3	4	5	6	7
8	9	10	11	12	13	14
15	16	17	18	19	20	21
...	...	...	...	...	...	...

Which region received the 1,986th rescue package? How many rescue packages had Region B received by the time the 1,976th package was handed out?

10. The sum of two numbers is 340. The quotient and remainder are 7 and 20 respectively when one of them is divided by the other. Find the two numbers.

280 60

290 50

300 40

11. A box of chocolates can be shared equally between two children. It can also be shared equally among 3, 4, 5 or 6 children. What is the minimum number of chocolates in the box?

978-1-62399-075-6

12. A number has a remainder of 2 when it is divided by 4. It also has a remainder of 2 when it is divided by 3. It has a remainder of 1 when it is divided by 7. Find the smallest possible value of this number.

6, 10, 14, 18, 22, 26, 30, 34, 38, 42, 46, 50

5, 8, 11, 14, 17, 20, 23, 26, 29, 32, 35, 38, 44, 50

8, 15, 22, 29, 36, 43, 50, 57, 64

978-1-62399-075-6
Singapore Math Challenge

13. The sum of a dividend, divisor, quotient and remainder is 171. The quotient and the remainder are 12 and 8 respectively.
Find the dividend and the divisor.

151

~~144 12~~

978-1-62399-075-6
Singapore Math Challenge

14. 160 beads are strung in this pattern: 5 red, 3 white, 4 black, 5 red, 3 white, 4 black, ... What color is the last bead? How many red beads are there?

978-1-62399-075-6
Singapore Math Challenge

15. Find the remainder and the last digit of the quotient of
$\underbrace{333 \ldots 333}_{12 \text{ digits}} \div 7$.

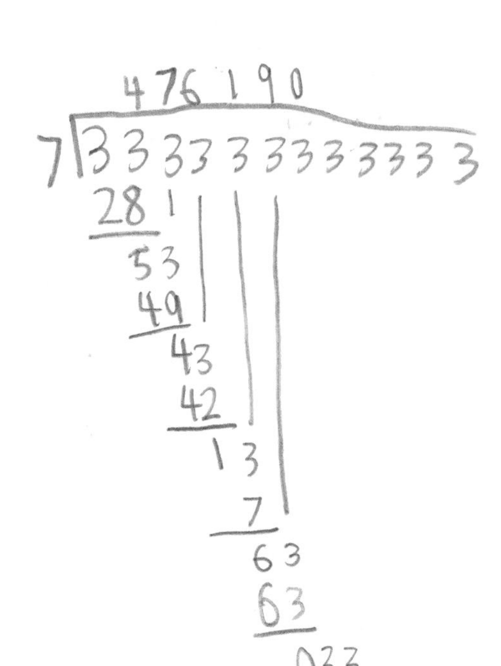

16. Find the remainder and the last digit of the quotient of

158730158730158730158730

7 | 111111111111111111111111

7
41
35
61
56
51
49
21
21

978-1-62399-075-6
Singapore Math Challenge

Average Problems

The concept of average is used extensively in our daily lives. For example, the average class score for a mathematics test or science exam, students' average height, etc.

The formulas to find average and total are shown below.

average = total ÷ number of units or events

total = average × number of units or events

An interesting fact about average is also shown below.

$1 + 2 + 3 + \ldots + 49 + 50 = $ (average of the first and last terms) × number of terms

978-1-62399-075-6
Singapore Math Challenge

Example 1: Daniel's average score for the first three tests in a year was 73. He worked very hard for the last test in that year to improve his average score to 75. What did he score on the last test to achieve this?

Solution:

Method 1: Solve by Reasoning

Total score for the first three tests = 3 × 73 = 219
Total score for the whole year = 4 × 75 = 300

300 – 219 = 81

Method 2: Solve by Drawing

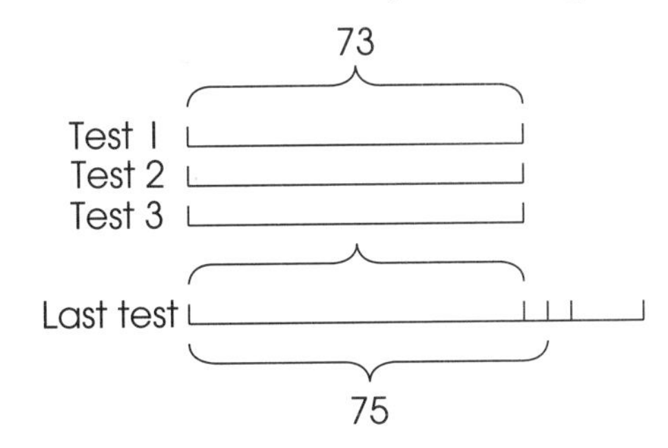

75 – 73 = 2
2 × 3 = 6
6 + 75 = 81

He scored an 81 on the last test.

978-1-62399-075-6
Singapore Math Challenge

Example 2: The sum of eight consecutive whole numbers is 188. List all eight numbers.

Solution:

$$188 \div 8 = 23.5$$

The first (and middle) pair of numbers are 23 and 24.

The eight numbers are 20, 21, 22, 23, 24, 25, 26 and 27.

978-1-62399-075-6
Singapore Math Challenge

Example 3: It took Samuel 18 min. to walk to the library at a speed of 40 m/min. He returned from the library at a walking speed of 60 m/min. What was his average speed for the whole trip?

Solution:

$$40 \times 18 = 720 \text{ m}$$

The library was 720 m away.

$$720 \div 60 = 12 \text{ min.}$$

He took 12 min. to return from the library.

$$18 + 12 = 30 \text{ min.}$$

He took 30 min. for the whole trip.

$$720 \times 2 = 1{,}440 \text{ m}$$

The total distance for the whole trip was 1,440 m.

$$1{,}440 \div 30 = 48$$

His average speed for the whole trip was 48 m/min.

978-1-62399-075-6
Singapore Math Challenge

Example 4: The average of A and B is 20. The average of B and C is 15. The average of C and D is 18. Find the average of A and D.

Solution:

$$\frac{A+B}{2} = 20$$

$$\frac{B+C}{2} = 15$$

$$\frac{C+D}{2} = 18$$

Simplifying all equations,

$A + B = 40$ .... (1)
$B + C = 30$ .... (2)
$C + D = 36$ .... (3)

(1) – (2)

$$A + B - (B + C) = 40 - 30$$
$$A + B - B - C = 10$$
$$A - C = 10 \quad \text{.......................... (4)}$$

(4) + (3)

$$A - C + C + D = 10 + 36$$
$$A + D = 46$$
$$\frac{A+D}{2} = 23$$

The average of A and D is 23.

978-1-62399-075-6
Singapore Math Challenge

1. The average mass of three people in an elevator was 60 kg. After another person boarded the elevator, the average mass became 57 kg. What was the mass of the last person?

57
× 4
228

978-1-62399-075-6
Singapore Math Challenge

2. The average of three numbers is 120. What number must be added so that the average will become 110?

3. The table below shows the test scores of six students.

Danny	Alison	Peter	John	Damien	Melissa
77	82	78	95	83	75

What is the average test score without considering the highest and the lowest scores?

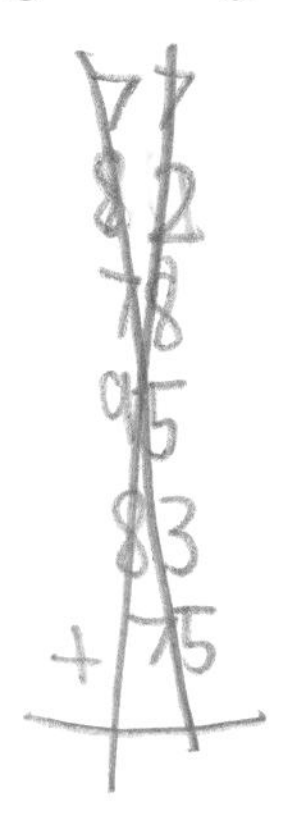

978-1-62399-075-6
Singapore Math Challenge

4. A box of thumbtacks weighed 1,590 grams. The box of thumbtacks weighed 1,470 grams after 40 thumbtacks were taken out from the box. How many thumbtacks were there in the box at first?

978-1-62399-075-6
Singapore Math Challenge

5. The average of five numbers is 20. The average of the five numbers is 18 when one of the numbers is changed to 4. What is the original value of the changed number?

6. The average of 35, 40, 41, m and 50 is 45.
Find the value of m.

225
−166
59

7. The average of A, B and C is 70. The value of A is 2 more than B. The value of B is 11 more than C.
Find the values of A, B and C.

78 76 65

~~76 74 61~~

75, 73, 62

978-1-62399-075-6
Singapore Math Challenge

8. Julie read 83 pages of a book on the first day, 66 pages on the second day, 74 pages on the third day and 73 pages on the fourth day. The number of pages she read on the fifth day was 12 pages more than the average number of pages she had read during the first four days. How many pages did she read on the fifth day?

83, 66, 74, 73

9. The average of A and B is 50. 100
The average of B and C is 43. 86
The average of A and C is 45. 90
Find the average of A, B and C.

54 46
53 47
55 45
57 43
52 48 38

52
48
+38
138

46

10. Joseph managed to read 83 pages of a book on day 1. He read another 65 pages, 60 pages and 84 pages of the same book on day 2, day 3 and day 4 respectively. On day 5, he read 8 pages more than the average number of pages he had read during the five days. How many pages of the book did he read on day 5?

83 65 60 84

11. The average mass of Ken, David and Eugene is 42 kg. David is 6 kg heavier than the average mass of Ken and Eugene. Ken is 6 kg heavier than Eugene. Find David's mass.

126

978-1-62399-075-6
Singapore Math Challenge

12. Matthew needs to get a perfect score of 100 for his last English test this year to improve his average score for the whole year from 84 to 86. How many English tests are there altogether in this year?

50

978-1-62399-075-6
Singapore Math Challenge

13. A car traveled from Town A to Town B at a speed of 30 km/h. The driver returned from Town B in the same car at a speed of 60 km/h. What was the average driving speed for the two trips?

978-1-62399-075-6
Singapore Math Challenge

14. The average of A and B is 8. The average of B and C is 3.6. The average of C and D is 5.8. Find the average of A and D.

11.6

10 6

6 1.2

1.2 10.4

978-1-62399-075-6
Singapore Math Challenge

15. The average mass of a group of children is 36 kg. If $\frac{3}{7}$ of the children are girls and their average mass is 32 kg, find the average mass of the boys.

36
× 7
252

252
− 96
156

39

Area

Area of square = side × side = $(\text{side})^2$ square unit

Area of rectangle = length × width square unit

Area of triangle = $\frac{1}{2}$ × base × height square unit

Area of trapezoid* = $\frac{1}{2}$ × (base 1 + base 2) × height square unit

*A trapezoid is a quadrilateral that has a pair of parallel sides.

Example 1:

The side of each square in the grid is 2 cm.
Find the area of the shaded region.

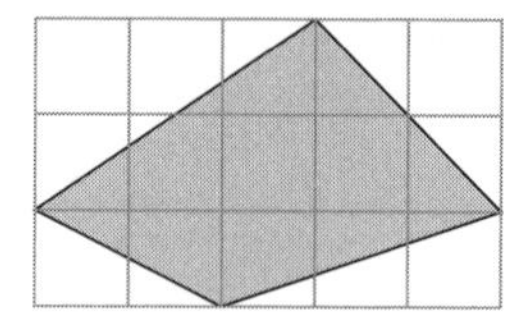

Solution:

Area of △A = $\frac{1}{2} \times 6 \times 4 = 12$ cm²

Area of △B = $\frac{1}{2} \times 4 \times 4 = 8$ cm²

Area of △C = $\frac{1}{2} \times 6 \times 2 = 6$ cm²

Area of △D = $\frac{1}{2} \times 4 \times 2 = 4$ cm²

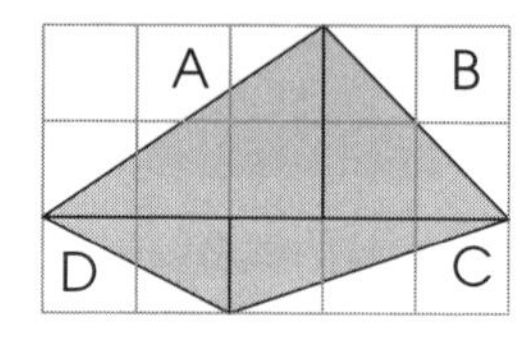

$12 + 8 + 6 + 4 = 30$ cm²

The area of the shaded region is 30 cm².

Example 2:

Find the area of the shaded region if A and B are squares with sides that are 5 cm and 8 cm respectively.

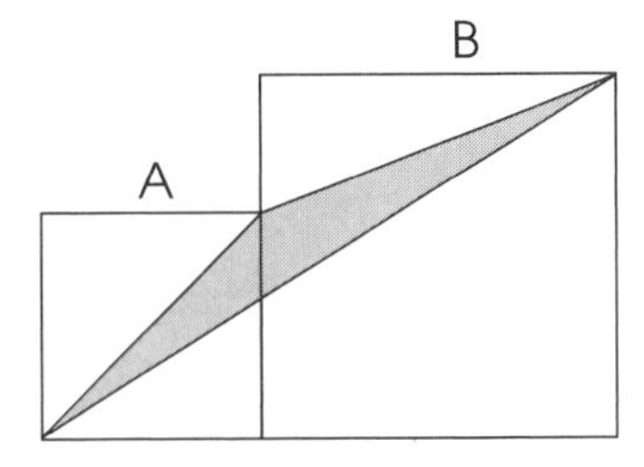

Solution:

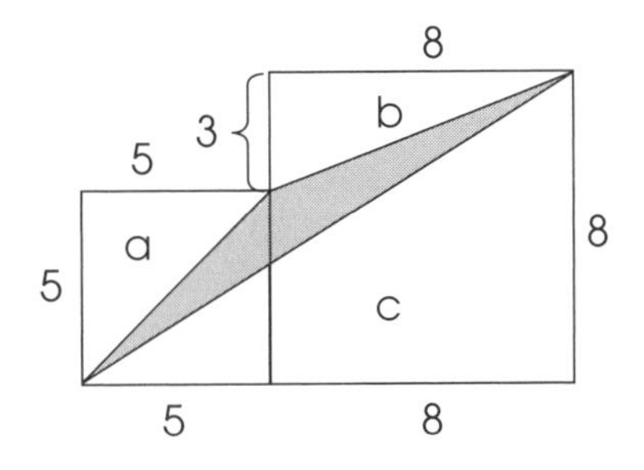

Area of $\triangle a = \frac{1}{2} \times 5 \times 5$

$= 12.5 \text{ cm}^2$

Area of $\triangle b = \frac{1}{2} \times 8 \times 3$

$= 12 \text{ cm}^2$

Area of $\triangle c = \frac{1}{2} \times (5 + 8) \times 8$

$= 52 \text{ cm}^2$

Total area of the two squares $= 5 \times 5 + 8 \times 8$

$= 25 + 64$

$= 89 \text{ cm}^2$

$89 - 12.5 - 12 - 52 = 12.5 \text{ cm}^2$

The area of the shaded region is 12.5 cm^2.

978-1-62399-075-6
Singapore Math Challenge

Example 3:

Line AE = Line EF = $\frac{1}{3}$ of Line AB.
Area of ΔADE = 5 cm^2.
If D is the midpoint of Line BC,
find the area of ΔABC.

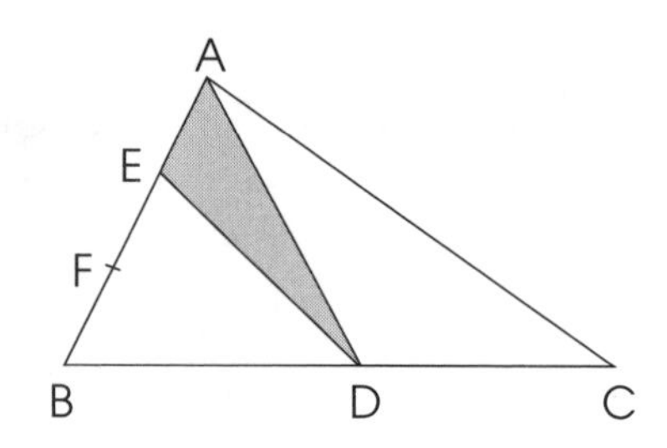

Solution:

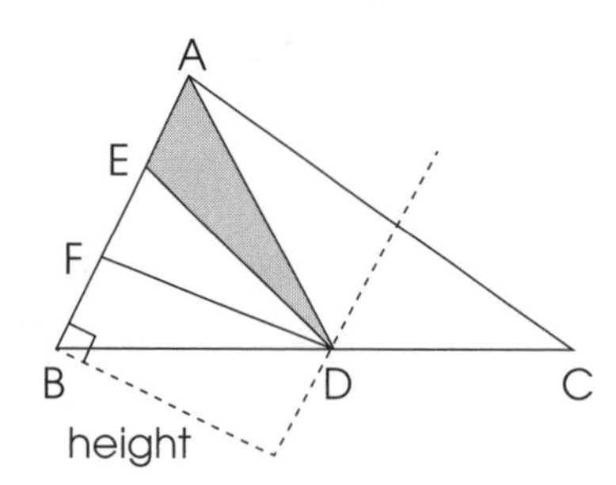

Area of ΔADE = Area of ΔEDF = Area of ΔFDB as they have the same base and same height.

Area of ΔABD = $3 \times 5 = 15$ cm^2

Area of ΔABD = Area of ΔADC as the base and the height of the two triangles are the same.

$15 \times 2 = 30$ cm^2

The area of ΔABC is 30 cm^2.

Example 4:

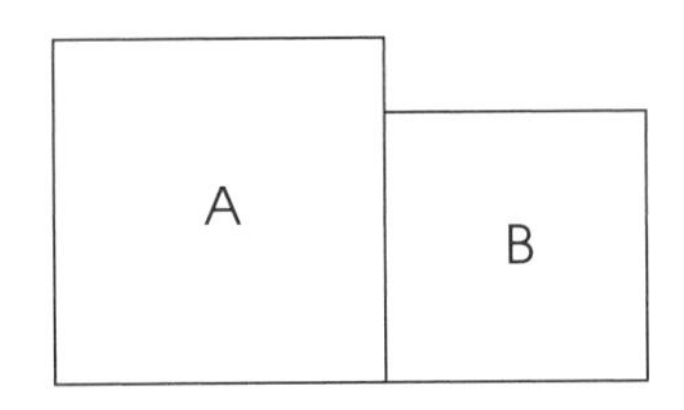

The sum of the areas of the two squares, A and B, is 202 cm^2.
Find the perimeter of the figure.

Solution:

First, make a list of the areas of different sides.

$2 \times 2 = 4\ cm^2$	$3 \times 3 = 9\ cm^2$
$4 \times 4 = 16\ cm^2$	$5 \times 5 = 25\ cm^2$
$6 \times 6 = 36\ cm^2$	$7 \times 7 = 49\ cm^2$
$8 \times 8 = 64\ cm^2$	$9 \times 9 = \textcircled{81}\ cm^2$
$10 \times 10 = 100\ cm^2$	$11 \times 11 = \textcircled{121}\ cm^2$

Next, we look for two numbers that will add up to 202.

$$81 + 121 = 202$$

The sides of the two squares measure 11 cm and 9 cm respectively.

$$11 \times 3 + 9 \times 3 + 11 - 9 = 62\ cm$$

The perimeter of the figure is 62 cm.

978-1-62399-075-6
Singapore Math Challenge

Example 5:

The base of a trapezoid is $\frac{2}{3}$ the length of its other base. The areas of the 2 triangles shown are 20 cm^2 and 24 cm^2.
Find the total area of the shaded regions.

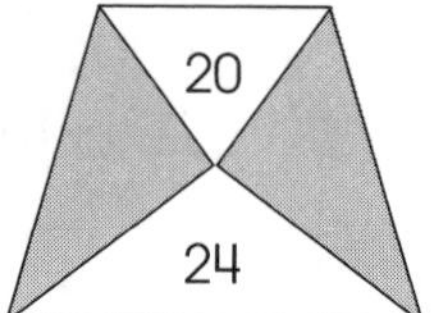

Solution:

A trapezoid has 2 parallel sides.
Let base AB be 2a, CD be 3a, and the heights of ΔABE and ΔCDE be h_1 and h_2 respectively.

Area of ΔABE: $20 = \frac{1}{2} \times 2a \times h_1$

$h_1 = \frac{20}{a}$

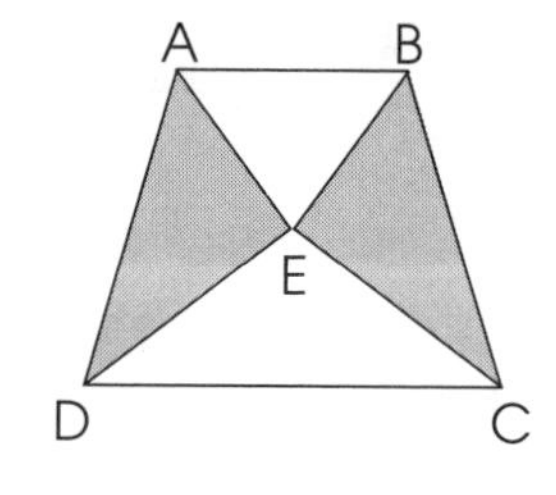

Area of ΔCDE: $24 = \frac{1}{2} \times 3a \times h_2$

$h_2 = \frac{16}{a}$

Using the formula,

$$(2a + 3a) \times (h_1 + h_2) \div 2 = 5a \times (\frac{20}{a} + \frac{16}{a}) \div 2$$

$$= 5a \times \frac{36}{a} \div 2$$

$$= \frac{36 \times 5}{2} = 90 \text{ cm}^2$$

The total area of the shaded regions is $90 - 20 - 24 = 46$ cm^2.

978-1-62399-075-6
Singapore Math Challenge

1. The side of each square in the grid is 1 cm. Find the total area of the shaded regions.

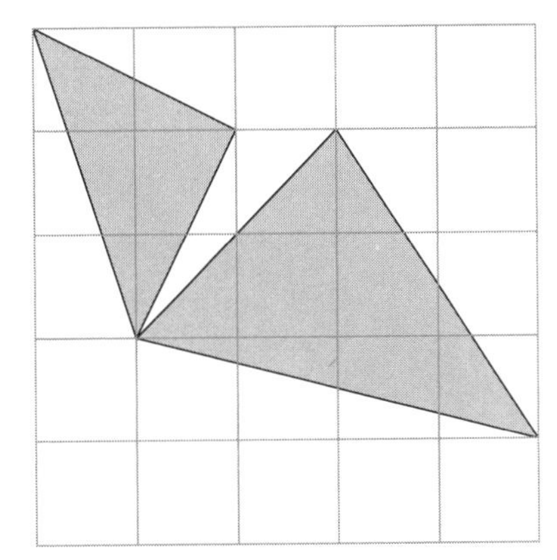

978-1-62399-075-6
Singapore Math Challenge

 Name ______________________ Date ____________

2. ABCD is a parallelogram. $\Delta EFG = 6\ cm^2$ and $DE = EF = \frac{1}{3} CD$. Find the area of ABCD.

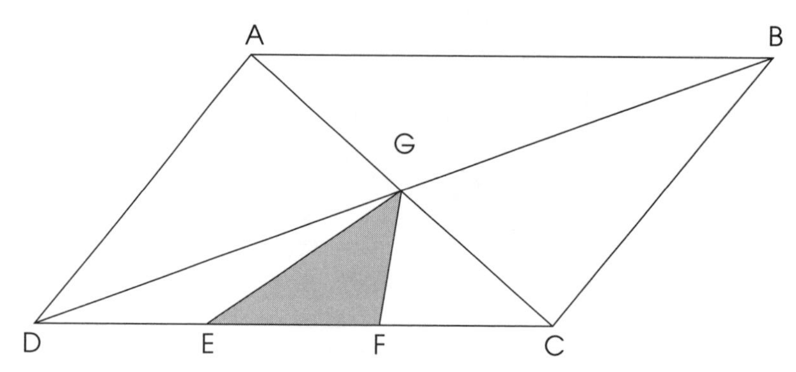

978-1-62399-075-6

3. The figure below is formed by two isoceles triangles. The bases of the triangles are 10 cm and 5 cm. Find the area of the shaded region.

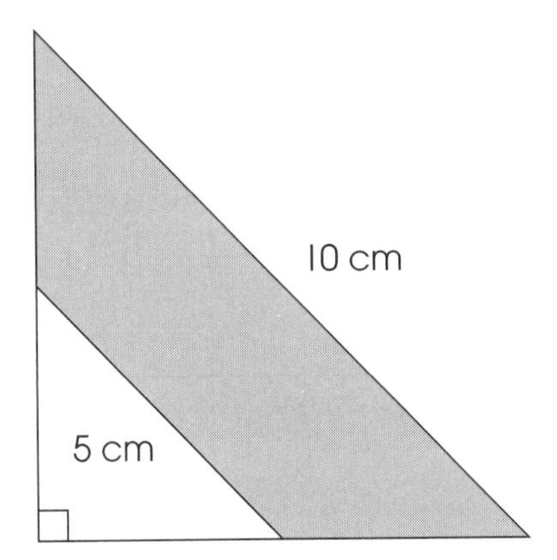

978-1-62399-075-6
Singapore Math Challenge

4. The difference in the areas of square A and square B is 95 cm^2. Find the perimeter of the figure.

A

B

1 2 3 4 5 6 7 8 9 10 11

1 4 9 16 25 36 49 64 81 100 121

978-1-62399-075-6
Singapore Math Challenge

5. ABCD is a square with sides that are 8 cm. AG = EC = 5 cm. Find the area of the shaded rectangle EFGH.

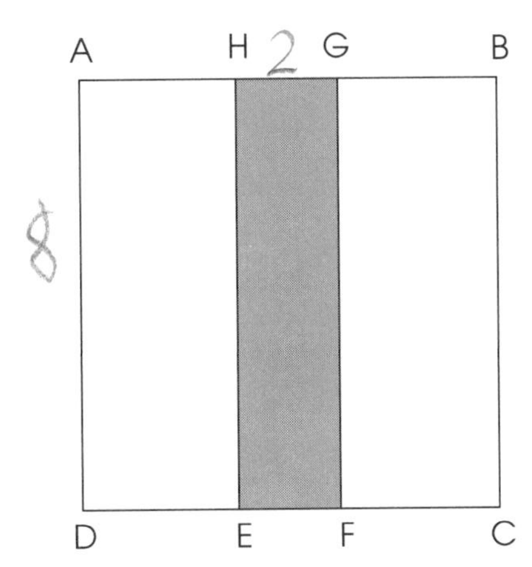

6. The figure below is made up of two squares with sides that are 5 cm and 3 cm. Find the area of the shaded region.

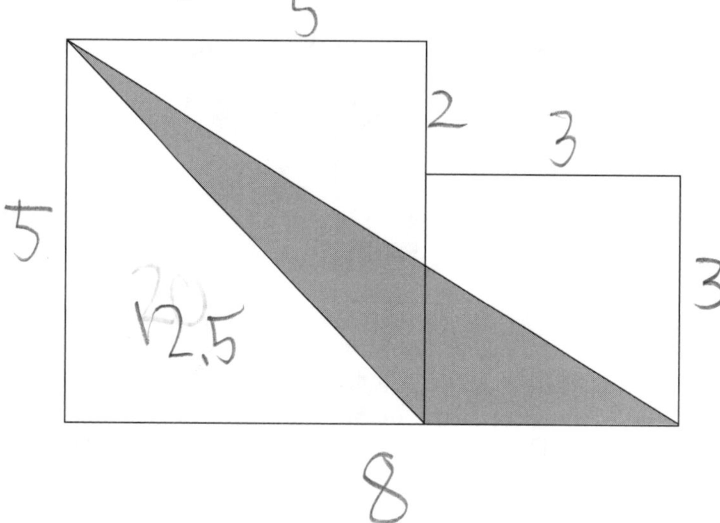

7. The figure below is formed by two squares with sides that are 6 cm and 4 cm. Find the area of the shaded region.

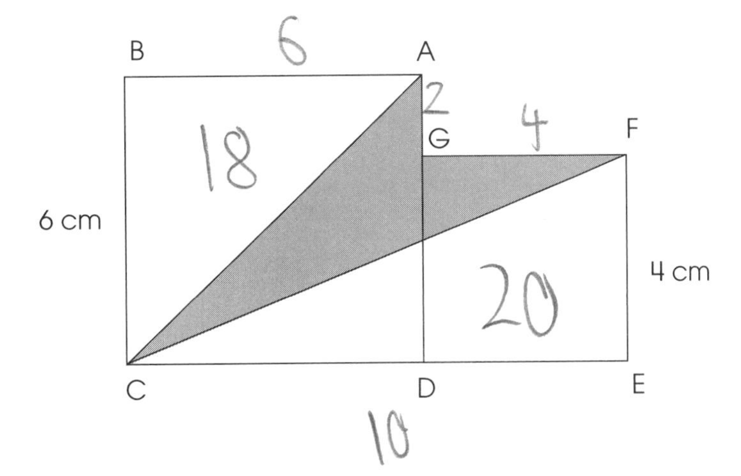

36
+16
52

52
−38
14

14

Name ______________________ Date ____________

8. Find the area of the rectangle that is embedded in the square.

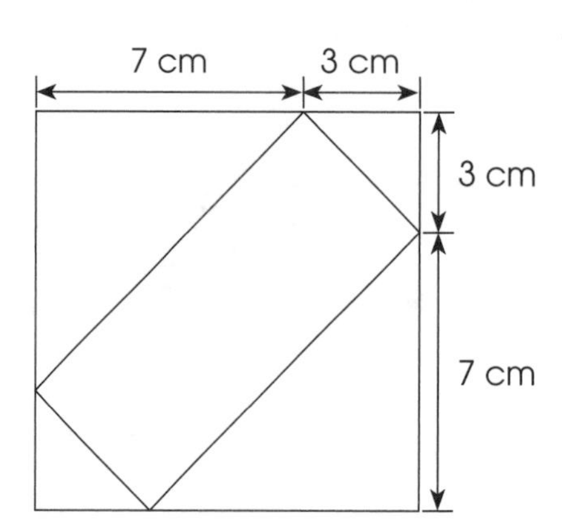

100

9. Find the area of the quadrilateral if AB = BC.

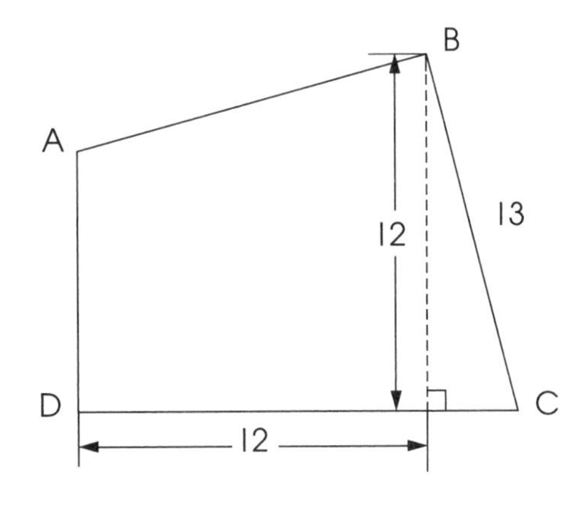

10. The diagram shows 6 squares, one inscribed in another at the midpoints. Find the area of the shaded region given that the side of the biggest square is 12 cm.

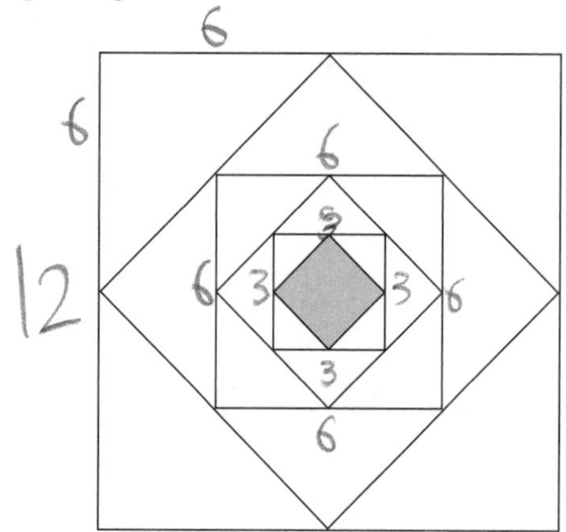

978-1-62399-075-6
Singapore Math Challenge

11. The diagram shows 3 squares, one inscribed in another at the midpoints. The smallest is subdivided into 9 equal squares. Given the area of $\Delta A = 4\ cm^2$, find the ratio of the total area of the shaded regions to that of the biggest square.

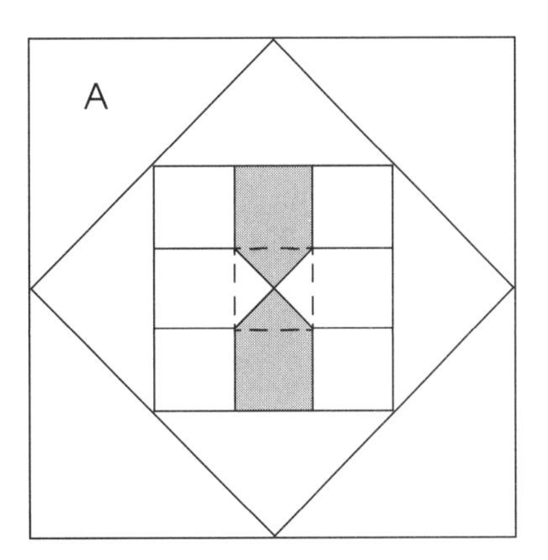

1 : 14.4

978-1-62399-075-6
Singapore Math Challenge

12. Two squares whose areas are x cm^2 and y cm^2 are embedded in square ABCD. The area of square ABCD is 252 cm^2. Find the values of x and y.

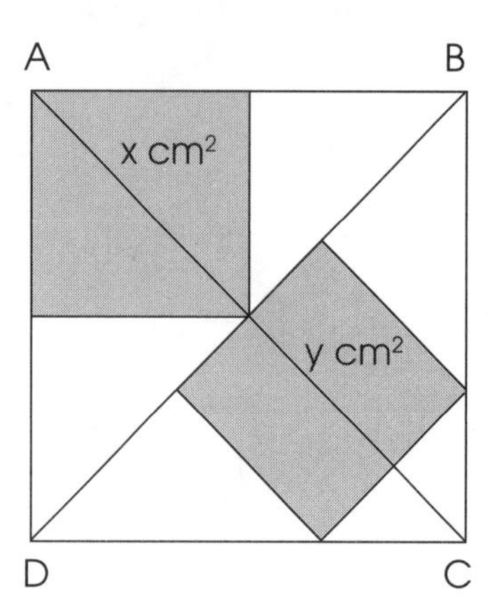

13. Two squares, A and B, overlap each other partially. Find the difference of the two shaded areas.

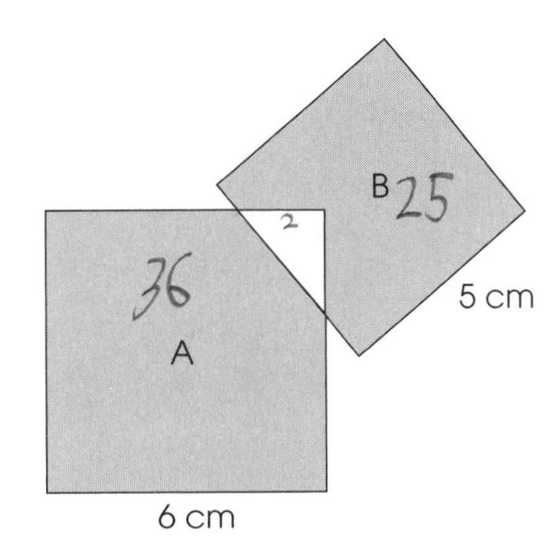

978-1-62399-075-6
Singapore Math Challenge

14. A plot of land has an area of 112. It is divided into 4 triangular plots, as shown. What is the area of the biggest plot of land? All units are in hectares.

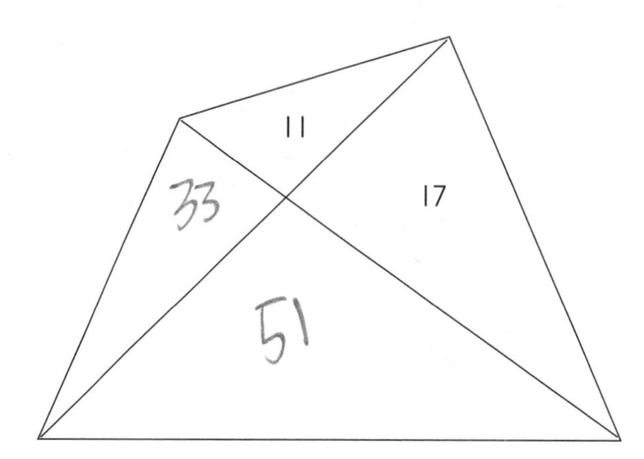

15. ABCD is a rectangle where BD is the diagonal. F is a point on AB and CF intersects BD at E. The areas of ΔBEF and ΔBEC are 20 cm^2 and 30 cm^2 respectively. Find the area of the quadrilateral ADEF.

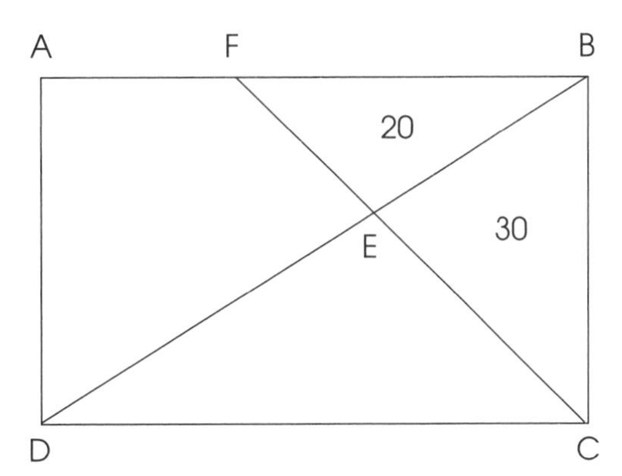

978-1-62399-075-6
Singapore Math Challenge

Name ______________________ Date __________

16. ABCD is a rectangle formed by five identical small rectangles. The width of each small rectangle is 6 cm. Find the perimeter of rectangle ABCD.

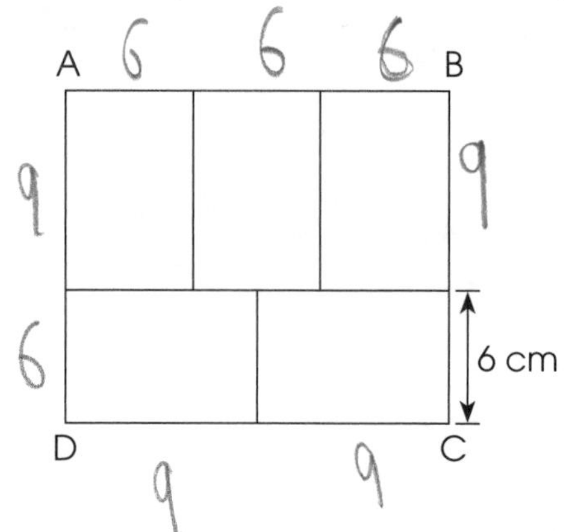

978-1-62399-075-6
Singapore Math Challenge

Fractions

Three important techniques related to fractions are explored in this chapter.

The first example in this chapter represents a sophisticated fraction. Problems of this nature are not particularly difficult; rather, they must be solved systematically and carefully in order to avoid unnecessary mistakes.

The technique of "Partial Fraction" is also introduced in this chapter. This technique allows a fraction to be expressed as a sum or difference of two fractions. Examples 2, 3 and 4 demonstrate the use of this technique to facilitate cancellation of identical fractions with different signs: the plus (+) sign and the minus (–) sign.

Last but not least, we sometimes represent a chunk of fractions by A and another chunk of fractions by B to simplify the problem. This helps us to solve extremely tedious problems involving fractions. This technique is demonstrated in Example 5.

978-1-62399-075-6
Singapore Math Challenge

Example 1: Evaluate $\cfrac{1}{1+\cfrac{1}{2+\cfrac{1}{3+\cfrac{1}{5}}}}$.

Solution:

Working upward, we begin with $\cfrac{1}{3+\cfrac{1}{5}}$.

$$\frac{1}{3+\frac{1}{5}} = \frac{1}{\frac{15+1}{5}} = \frac{1}{\frac{16}{5}} = \frac{5}{16}$$

$$2 + \frac{5}{16} = \frac{32+5}{16} = \frac{37}{16}$$

$$\frac{1}{\frac{37}{16}} = \frac{16}{37}$$

$$\cfrac{1}{1+\cfrac{1}{2+\cfrac{1}{3+\cfrac{1}{5}}}} = \frac{1}{1+\frac{16}{37}} = \frac{1}{\frac{37+16}{37}} = \frac{1}{\frac{53}{37}} = \frac{37}{53}$$

978-1-62399-075-6
Singapore Math Challenge

Example 2: Evaluate $\frac{1}{1 \times 2} + \frac{1}{2 \times 3} + \frac{1}{3 \times 4} + \ldots + \frac{1}{99 \times 100}$.

Solution:

We can rewrite each term as shown below.

$$\frac{1}{1 \times 2} = 1 - \frac{1}{2}$$

$$\frac{1}{2 \times 3} = \frac{1}{6} = \frac{3-2}{6} = \frac{3}{6} - \frac{2}{6} = \frac{1}{2} - \frac{1}{3}$$

$$\frac{1}{3 \times 4} = \frac{1}{12} = \frac{4-3}{12} = \frac{4}{12} - \frac{3}{12} = \frac{1}{3} - \frac{1}{4}$$

$$\vdots$$

$$\frac{1}{99 \times 100} = \frac{1}{9{,}900} = \frac{100-99}{9{,}900} = \frac{1}{99} - \frac{1}{100}$$

$$\frac{1}{1 \times 2} + \frac{1}{2 \times 3} + \frac{1}{3 \times 4} + \ldots + \frac{1}{99 \times 100}$$

$$1 - \cancel{\frac{1}{2}} + \cancel{\frac{1}{2}} - \cancel{\frac{1}{3}} + \cancel{\frac{1}{3}} - \cancel{\frac{1}{4}} + \ldots + \cancel{\frac{1}{99}} - \frac{1}{100}$$

$$= 1 - \frac{1}{100}$$

$$= \frac{99}{100}$$

As a general rule, we can express each term in a series of fractions with the form of $\frac{1}{n(n+1)}$ into $\frac{1}{n} - \frac{1}{n+1}$.

(1) $\frac{1}{n(n+1)} = \frac{1}{n} - \frac{1}{n+1}$

It follows,

(2) $\frac{1}{n(n+d)} = \frac{1}{d} \times (\frac{1}{n} - \frac{1}{n+d})$

Example 3: Evaluate $\frac{1}{1 \times 4} + \frac{1}{4 \times 7} + \frac{1}{7 \times 10} + \frac{1}{10 \times 13} + \ldots + \frac{1}{97 \times 100}$.

Solution:

$$\frac{1}{1 \times 4} + \frac{1}{4 \times 7} + \frac{1}{7 \times 10} + \frac{1}{10 \times 13} + \ldots + \frac{1}{97 \times 100}$$

$$= \frac{1}{3} \times (1 - \frac{1}{4} + \frac{1}{4} - \frac{1}{7} + \frac{1}{7} + \frac{1}{10} - \frac{1}{10} - \frac{1}{13} \ldots + \frac{1}{97} - \frac{1}{100})$$

$$= \frac{1}{3} \times (1 - \frac{1}{100})$$

$$= \frac{1}{3_1} \times \frac{99^{33}}{100}$$

$$= \frac{33}{100}$$

Example 4: Evaluate $1 - \frac{5}{6} + \frac{7}{12} - \frac{9}{20} + \frac{11}{30} - \frac{13}{42} + \frac{15}{56} - \frac{17}{72} + \frac{19}{90}$.

Analysis: Each term can be expressed as a sum of two fractions.

$$\frac{5}{6} = \frac{1}{2} + \frac{1}{3}$$

$$\frac{7}{12} = \frac{1}{3} + \frac{1}{4}$$

$$\vdots$$

$$\frac{19}{90} = \frac{1}{9} + \frac{1}{10}$$

Solution:

$$1 - \frac{5}{6} + \frac{7}{12} - \frac{9}{20} + \frac{11}{30} - \frac{13}{42} + \frac{15}{56} - \frac{17}{72} + \frac{19}{90}$$

$$= 1 - (\frac{1}{2} + \frac{1}{3}) + (\frac{1}{3} + \frac{1}{4}) - (\frac{1}{4} + \frac{1}{5}) + \dots + (\frac{1}{9} + \frac{1}{10})$$

$$= 1 - \frac{1}{2} - \cancel{\frac{1}{3}} + \cancel{\frac{1}{3}} + \cancel{\frac{1}{4}} - \cancel{\frac{1}{4}} - \cancel{\frac{1}{5}} + \dots + \cancel{\frac{1}{9}} + \frac{1}{10}$$

$$= 1 - \frac{1}{2} + \frac{1}{10}$$

$$= \frac{1}{2} + \frac{1}{10}$$

$$= \frac{6}{10}$$

$$= \frac{3}{5}$$

978-1-62399-075-6
Singapore Math Challenge

Example 5: Evaluate $(1 + \frac{1}{31} + \frac{1}{41} + \frac{1}{51}) \times (\frac{1}{31} + \frac{1}{41} + \frac{1}{51} + \frac{1}{61}) -$

$$(1 + \frac{1}{31} + \frac{1}{41} + \frac{1}{51} + \frac{1}{61}) \times (\frac{1}{31} + \frac{1}{41} + \frac{1}{51}).$$

Analysis: The trick to this question is simplification.

Let A be $\frac{1}{31} + \frac{1}{41} + \frac{1}{51}$ and B be $\frac{1}{31} + \frac{1}{41} + \frac{1}{51} + \frac{1}{61}$.

Solution:

By substitution, we have

$(1 + A) \times B - (1 + B) \times A$.

Recall $a \times (b + c) = a \times b + a \times c$.

$(1 + A) \times B - (1 + B) \times A$

$= B + AB - (A + AB)$

$= B + \cancel{AB} - A - \cancel{AB}$

$= B - A$

$= (\cancel{\frac{1}{31}} + \cancel{\frac{1}{41}} + \cancel{\frac{1}{51}} + \frac{1}{61}) - (\cancel{\frac{1}{31}} + \cancel{\frac{1}{41}} + \cancel{\frac{1}{51}})$

$= \frac{1}{61}$

978-1-62399-075-6
Singapore Math Challenge

1. Evaluate $\dfrac{1}{2+\dfrac{1}{3+\dfrac{1}{4+\dfrac{1}{5}}}}$.

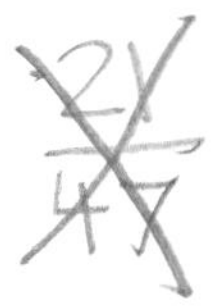

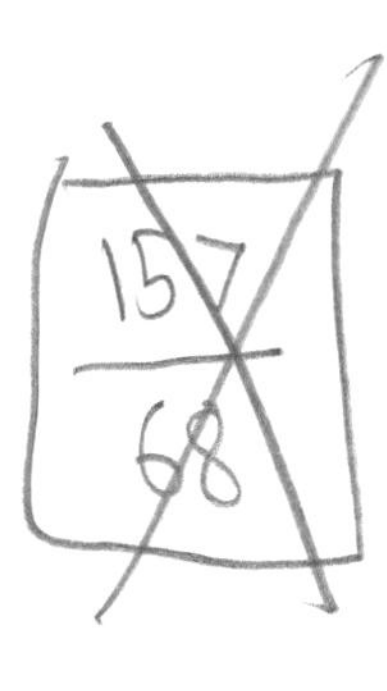

 Name ________________ Date ________

2. Evaluate $\dfrac{1 + \dfrac{1}{2 - \dfrac{1}{4}}}{1 + \dfrac{1}{1 + \dfrac{1}{3}}}$.

$\dfrac{1 + \dfrac{1}{\frac{7}{4}}}{1 + \dfrac{1}{\frac{4}{3}}}$

$\dfrac{1 + \frac{4}{7}}{1 + \frac{3}{4}}$

$\dfrac{\frac{11}{7}}{\frac{7}{4}}$

$\dfrac{\frac{44}{28}}{\frac{49}{28}}$

$\boxed{\dfrac{44}{49}}$

3. Evaluate $\dfrac{1}{4 + \dfrac{1}{3 - \dfrac{1}{2 + \dfrac{1}{7}}}}$.

$\frac{15}{7}$ $3 - \frac{7}{15}$

$2\frac{8}{15}$ $\frac{38}{15}$

$\frac{15}{38}$ $\frac{38}{167}$

978-1-62399-075-6
Singapore Math Challenge

4. Evaluate $1\frac{1}{3} - \frac{7}{12} + \frac{9}{20} - \frac{11}{30} + \frac{13}{42} - \frac{15}{56} + \frac{17}{72}$.

$\frac{4}{3} - \frac{7}{12} + \frac{9}{20}$

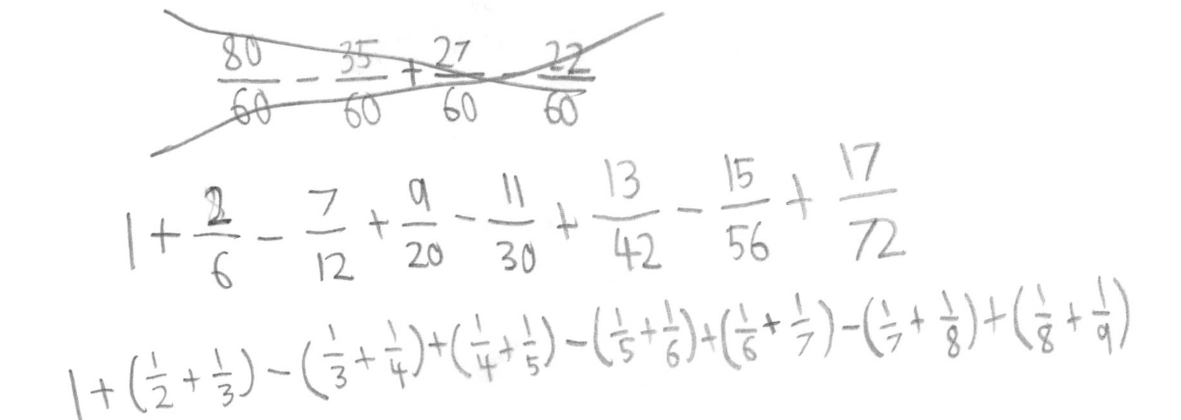

$1 + \frac{1}{2} + \frac{1}{9}$

$1 + \frac{9}{18} + \frac{2}{18}$

$1 + \frac{11}{18}$

$\frac{29}{18}$

978-1-62399-075-6
Singapore Math Challenge

5. Evaluate $\frac{1}{2} + \frac{5}{6} + \frac{11}{12} + \frac{19}{20} + \ldots + \frac{89}{90}$.

$\frac{1}{2}$ $\frac{5}{6}$ $\frac{11}{12}$ $\frac{19}{20}$ $\frac{29}{30}$ $\frac{41}{42}$ $\frac{55}{56}$ $\frac{71}{72}$ $\frac{89}{90}$

$\frac{6}{12}$ $\frac{10}{12}$ $\frac{11}{12}$

$\frac{30}{60}$ $\frac{50}{60}$ $\frac{55}{60}$ $\frac{57}{60}$ $\frac{58}{60}$

978-1-62399-075-6
Singapore Math Challenge

6. Evaluate $\frac{1}{1 \times 5} + \frac{1}{5 \times 9} + \frac{1}{9 \times 13} + \ldots + \frac{1}{97 \times 101}$.

$\frac{1}{4} \times \frac{100}{101}$

978-1-62399-075-6
Singapore Math Challenge

7. Evaluate $(\frac{1}{2} + \frac{1}{3} + \ldots + \frac{1}{10}) + (\frac{2}{3} + \frac{2}{4} + \ldots + \frac{2}{10}) + (\frac{3}{4} + \ldots + \frac{3}{10}) + \ldots + (\frac{8}{9} + \frac{8}{10}) + \frac{9}{10}$.

8. Evaluate $\frac{1}{3} + \frac{1}{15} + \frac{1}{35} + \frac{1}{63} + \frac{1}{99} + \frac{1}{143} + \frac{1}{195}$.

978-1-62399-075-6
Singapore Math Challenge

9. Evaluate $(\frac{1}{2} + \frac{2}{3} + \frac{3}{4} + \frac{4}{5})^2 + (\frac{1}{2} + \frac{2}{3} + \frac{3}{4} + \frac{4}{5}) \times \frac{1}{2} - (1 + \frac{1}{2} + \frac{2}{3} + \frac{3}{4} + \frac{4}{5}) \times (\frac{2}{3} + \frac{3}{4} + \frac{4}{5})$.

978-1-62399-075-6
Singapore Math Challenge

 Name ____________________ Date __________

10. Evaluate $\frac{2{,}007 + 2{,}006 \times 2{,}008}{2{,}007 \times 2{,}008 - 1}$.

978-1-62399-075-6
Singapore Math Challenge

11. Evaluate $\frac{1}{2,008} + \frac{2}{2,008} + \frac{3}{2,008} + \ldots + \frac{2,006}{2,008} + \frac{2,007}{2,008}$.

978-1-62399-075-6
Singapore Math Challenge

12. Evaluate $\frac{1}{2,007} + \frac{2}{2,007} - \frac{3}{2,007} - \frac{4}{2,007} + \frac{5}{2,007} + \frac{6}{2,007} - \frac{7}{2,007} - \frac{8}{2,007} + \frac{9}{2,007} + \frac{10}{2,007} - \ldots - \frac{2,004}{2,007} + \frac{2,005}{2,007} + \frac{2,006}{2,007}$.

978-1-62399-075-6
Singapore Math Challenge

13. Evaluate $\frac{2,000}{1 \times 2} + \frac{2,000}{2 \times 3} + \frac{2,000}{3 \times 4} + \dots + \frac{2,000}{1,999 \times 2,000}$.

978-1-62399-075-6

14. Evaluate $\frac{1}{1+2} + \frac{1}{1+2+3} + \frac{1}{1+2+3+4} + \ldots + \frac{1}{1+2+3+\ldots+50}$.

Square Numbers and Value of Ones Digit

(A) Square Numbers: The product of a whole number and itself is called a square number.

Examples:

$1 \times 1 = 1^2 = 1$
$2 \times 2 = 2^2 = 4$
$3 \times 3 = 3^2 = 9$
$4 \times 4 = 4^2 = 16$
$5 \times 5 = 5^2 = 25$

If we are to put it in diagrammatic form, a square number represents the area of a square.

Important note: The digit in the ones place of a square number can only be either 1, 4, 5, 6, 9 or 0.

Numbers that end with 2, 3, 7 and 8 are not squares of any numbers.

978-1-62399-075-6
Singapore Math Challenge

Example 1: List all the square numbers that are larger than 200 but smaller than 400.

Analysis:

We are looking for numbers which are multiples of themselves and whose products are between 200 and 400.

Solution:

$$14 \times 14 = 196$$

The square number, 196, is not within the range.

$$20 \times 20 = 400$$

The square number, 200, is also not within the range.

So, the square numbers of 15, 16, 17, 18 and 19 are within the range.

$$15^2 = 225$$
$$16^2 = 256$$
$$17^2 = 289$$
$$18^2 = 324$$
$$19^2 = 361$$

The square numbers that are larger than 200 but smaller than 400 are 225, 256, 289, 324 and 361.

978-1-62399-075-6
Singapore Math Challenge

Example 2: Which of the following numbers are square numbers?

3,647, 6,889, 3,048, 5,625

Analysis:

All square numbers will end with digits 1, 4, 5, 6, 9 or 0.
We can therefore rule out 3,647 and 3,048.

Solution:

For 6,889, the last digit of the 2-digit square root must be either 3 or 7.

$80 \times 80 = 6{,}400$ (we can make an estimate)
$83 \times 83 = 6{,}889$
$87 \times 87 = 7{,}569$

6,889 is a square number.

For 5,625, the last digit must be 5.

$70 \times 70 = 4{,}900$ (we can make an estimate)
$75 \times 75 = 5{,}625$

5,625 is also a square number.

978-1-62399-075-6
Singapore Math Challenge

Example 3: The product of a whole number, m, and 7,920 is a square number. Find the smallest possible value of m.

Solution:

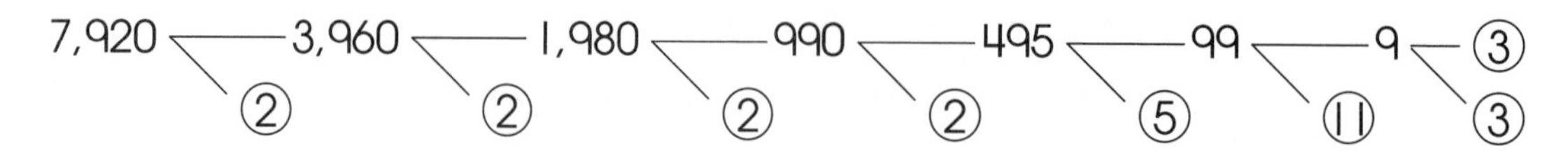

$7{,}920 = 2 \times 2 \times 2 \times 2 \times 3 \times 3 \times 5 \times 11$

To make two identical numbers from 7,920, we add prime numbers to make it "balanced."

$7{,}920 \times m = 2 \times 2 \times 2 \times 2 \times 3 \times 3 \times 5 \times 5 \times 11 \times 11$

$m = 5 \times 11 = 55$

The smallest possible value of m is 55.

(B) Value of the Ones Digit: To find the value of the ones digit, it is important to observe how the ones digit changes with each multiplication.

We have, $5^5 = 5 \times 5 \times 5 \times 5 \times 5$

Likewise, $2^8 = 2 \times 2 \times 2 \times 2 \times 2 \times 2 \times 2 \times 2$

The number written in superscript is the number of times the number multiplies itself.

978-1-62399-075-6
Singapore Math Challenge

Example 4: Find the values of the ones digits of

(a) 5^{10}

Power of 5	5^1	5^2	5^3	...	...	...
Value of ones digit	5	5	5	...	...	...

The value of the ones digit of 5^{10} is 5.

(b) 8^{25}

Power of 8	8^1	8^2	8^3	8^4	8^5	8^6	...
Value of ones digit	8	4	2	6	8	4	...

The ones digit recurs in the following pattern:

8, 4, 2, 6, 8, 4, 2, 6, ...
R1 R2 R3 R0

$25 \div 4 = 6$ R 1

The value of the ones digit of 8^{25} is 8.

978-1-62399-075-6
Singapore Math Challenge

(c) 9^{99}

Power of 8	9^1	9^2	9^3	9^4	9^5	...	...	...
Value of ones digit	9	1	9	1	9	...	...	...

The ones digit recurs in the following pattern:

9, 1, 9, 1, 9, 1, ...
R1 R0

$99 \div 2 = 49$ R 1

The value of the ones digit of 9^{99} is 9.

(d) $4^{1,999}$

Power of 4	4^1	4^2	4^3	4^4	4^5	4^6	...
Value of ones digit	4	6	4	6	4	6	...

The ones digit recurs in the following pattern:

4, 6, 4, 6, ...
R1 R0

$1,999 \div 2 = 999$ R 1

The value of the ones digit of $4^{1,999}$ is 4.

Example 5: Beginning from the ones digit, how many consecutive zeros are there in 625×64?

Solution:

$$2 \times 5 = 10$$

Each pair of (2, 5) gives a zero.

$625 = 5 \times 5 \times 5 \times 5$
$64 = 2 \times 2 \times 2 \times 2 \times 2 \times 2$

There are 4 consecutive zeros in 625×64.

978-1-62399-075-6
Singapore Math Challenge

 Name ______________________ Date ____________

1. Test to see if it is possible for each of the following numbers to be a square number. Find the smallest possible value of the number if it is indeed a square number.

(a) ab7

(b) mn8

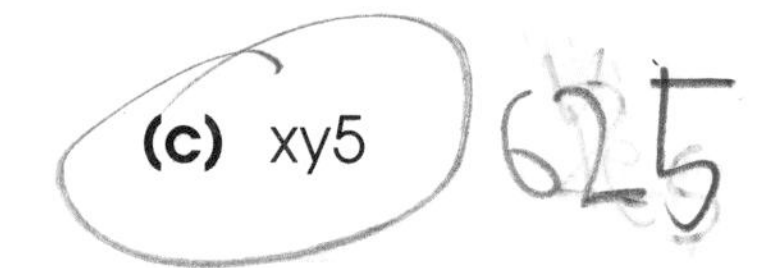

(c) xy5

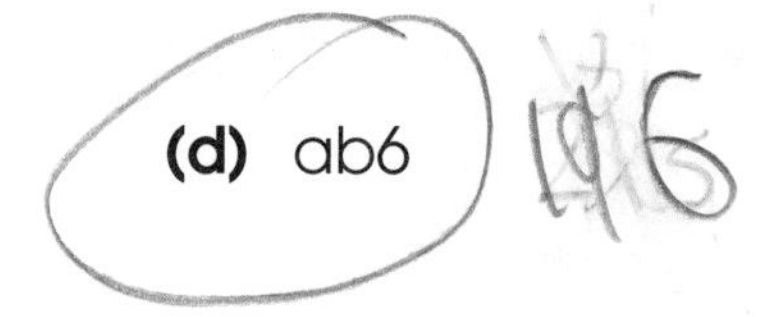

(d) ab6

2. Which of the following are square numbers?

(a) 2,209 Yes

(b) 3,402 No

(c) 3,136

275
275
3025

Yes

(d) 5,041

978-1-62399-075-6
Singapore Math Challenge

3. The digits 0 and 1 can occur in the ones place of a square number, like $9 \times 9 = 81$ and $10 \times 10 = 100$. The digit 2 cannot occur in the ones place of any square number. What other numbers can occur in the ones place of a square number?

978-1-62399-075-6

4. List all the square numbers that are larger than 300 but smaller than 500.

two more

324
361
400
441
484

5. The product of 2,100 and a whole number, m, is a square number. Find the smallest possible value of m.

6. The product of David's grandfather's and David's father's ages is 2,268. The product of his grandfather's, his father's and David's ages is a square number. How old is each?

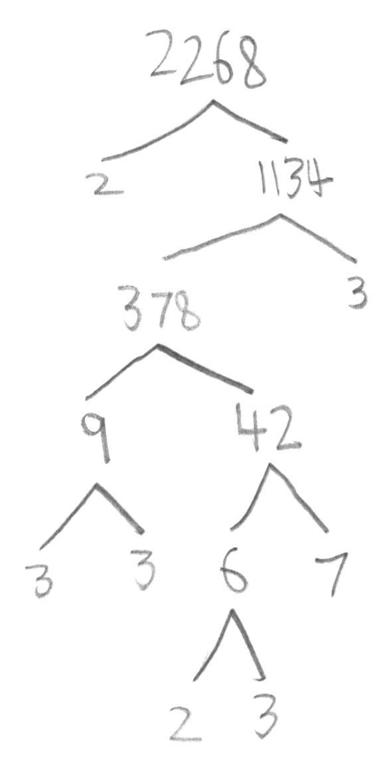

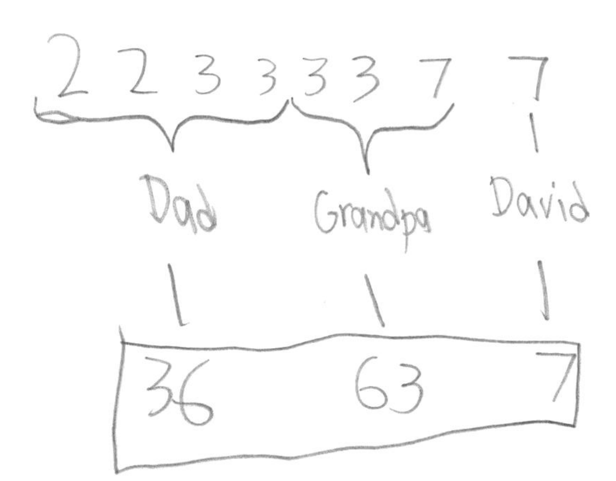

 Name ______________________ Date ____________

7. The product of 1,815 and m is a square number. Find the smallest possible value of m.

978-1-62399-075-6
Singapore Math Challenge

8. The area of the figure formed by 3 squares, A, B and C, is 142 cm^2. Find the lengths of the sides of each square.

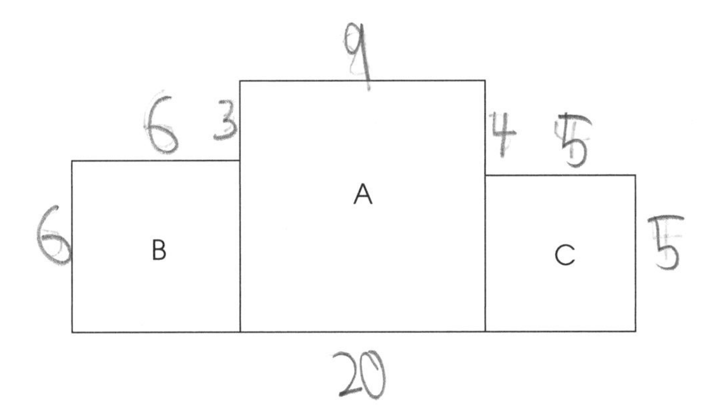

978-1-62399-075-6
Singapore Math Challenge

9. The number of students in Woodsville Elementary School in the year 2005 was a square number. The number of students in the year 2006 was also a square number and it was 101 more than the number of students in 2005. What was the number of students in the year 2006?

51
x 51
51
255
2601

978-1-62399-075-6
Singapore Math Challenge

10. Find the values of the ones digits of the following.

(a) 26^{62}

(b) 33^{303}

978-1-62399-075-6
Singapore Math Challenge

(c) 124^{15}

(d) 19^{91}

11. Find the values of the last digits of the following.

(a) 2^{30}

2 4 8 6

(b) $3^{2,000}$

3 9 7 1

978-1-62399-075-6
Singapore Math Challenge

(c) $7^{2,002}$

7 9 3 1

9

(d) 99^{99}

12. (a) What is the value of the ones digit of $27^{2,000}$?

(b) What is the value of the ones digit in $2^{216,091} - 1$?

978-1-62399-075-6
Singapore Math Challenge

13. Compute the value of the ones digit in

$$1,999 \times 2,001 \times 2,003 \times 2,005 \times 2,007 - 2,000 \times 2,002 \times 2,004 \times 2,006.$$

105
× 9
945

945 − 48 = 897

978-1-62399-075-6
Singapore Math Challenge

14. Find the sum of the values of the ones digits of 78^{87} and 87^{78}.

8 4 2 6

2 9

978-1-62399-075-6
Singapore Math Challenge

15. If we write 1,001 continuously for 1,001 times to form a number, what will be the remainder when such a number is divided by 11?

16. How many consecutive zeros, beginning from the ones digit, are there in

$$1 \times 2 \times 3 \times 4 \times 5 \times \ldots \times 99 \times 100?$$

978-1-62399-075-6
Singapore Math Challenge

 Name ______________________ Date ____________

17. Find the ones digit in

$$1^5 + 2^9 + 3^{13} + 4^{17} + 5^{21} + 6^{25} + 7^{29} + 8^{33} + 9^{37} + 10^{41}.$$

1 2 3 4 5 6 7 8 9 0

978-1-62399-075-6

18. Given
$$1! = 1$$
$$2! = 1 \times 2$$
$$3! = 1 \times 2 \times 3$$
$$\vdots$$
$$n! = 1 \times 2 \times 3 \times \ldots \times n$$

Find the last 2 digits in

$$1! + 2! + 3! + \ldots + 99!$$

978-1-62399-075-6
Singapore Math Challenge

Percentage

This chapter aims to expose students to various types of percentage problems, combined with different topics. For example, a percentage problem is often combined with the topic of ratio. Another combination is the presence of percentage in speed problems.

This chapter also introduces students to bar charts and pie charts. Students who are able to write simple equations may also find it very useful.

978-1-62399-075-6

Example 1: The wholesale cost of a TV is \$4,800. At the store, it is marked at 20% above its wholesale cost, but later sold at 75% of its retail price. What is the amount of loss?

Solution:

Retail price = 4,800 × (100% + 20%)
= 4,800 × 120%
= 4,800 × 1.2, as $\frac{120}{100} = 1.2$
= \$5,760

Actual selling price = 5,760 × 75%
= 5,760 × 0.75, as $\frac{75}{100} = 0.75$
= \$4,320

4,800 – 4,320 = \$480

The amount of loss is \$480.

978-1-62399-075-6
Singapore Math Challenge

Example 2: The base of a triangle is increased by 10% and its height is increased by 20%. Find the new area of the triangle as a percentage of the original one.

Solution:

Let b and h be the base and height of the triangle respectively.

New base $= b \times (100\% + 10\%)$

$= b \times 1.1$, as $110\% = \frac{110}{100}$

$= 1.1 \times b$

New height $= h \times (100\% + 20\%)$

$= h \times 1.2$

$= 1.2 \times b$

Area of $\Delta = \frac{1}{2} \times b \times h$

$$\frac{\frac{1}{2} \times 1.1 \times b \times 1.2 \times h}{\frac{1}{2} \times b \times h} \times 100\%$$

$= 1.1 \times 1.2 \times 100\%$

$= 132\%$

The area of the new triangle is 132% of the original one.

978-1-62399-075-6
Singapore Math Challenge

Example 3: 60% of the marbles in a container are red and the rest are black. After another 9 black marbles are added, the ratio of red and black marbles becomes 4 : 3. How many black marbles are there now?

Solution:

At first, $r : b = 60\% : 40\% = 3 : 2$

$$\frac{r}{b} = \frac{3}{2}$$

$$2r = 3b \quad \text{.........................} \ (1)$$

Later, $r : b + 9 = 4 : 3$

$$\frac{r}{b+9} = \frac{4}{3}$$

$$3r = 4 \times (b + 9)$$

$$3r = 4b + 36 \quad \text{.........................} \ (2)$$

$(1) \times 3$

$$6r = 9b \quad \text{.........................} \ (3)$$

$(2) \times 2$

$$6r = 8b + 72 \quad \text{.........................} \ (4)$$

Equate (3) and (4)

$$9b = 8b + 72$$

$$b = 72$$

$$72 + 9 = 81$$

There are 81 black marbles now.

978-1-62399-075-6
Singapore Math Challenge

Example 4: An admission ticket to a football game costs \$15. The number of spectators goes up by 100% when the ticket price reduces. If ticket sales go up by 20%, how much is a ticket now?

Solution:

Suppose there are 100 spectators at first.
Ticket sales are $100 \times \$15 = \$1,500$

Ticket sales now become $1,500 \times \frac{120}{100}$

$= 1,500 \times \frac{6}{5}$

$= \$1,800$ after adjustment in ticket price.

So, there must be 200 spectators.

$1,800 \div 200 = \$9$

Each ticket costs \$9 now.

978-1-62399-075-6

Example 5: A car is traveling from Town A to Town B. If the speed of the car is increased by 20%, it will reach the destination 1 hour earlier. What must be the increase in the car's speed in percentage if it is to reach the destination 2 hours earlier?

Solution:

Method 1: Guess and Check

Suppose the car's speed is 80 km/h.

$80 \times 120\% = 96$ km/h

$80 \times 6 = 480$ km

$96 \times 5 = 480$ km

480 km is the hypothetical distance.

$6 - 4 = 2$ hours earlier

The car must travel at $480 \div 4 = 120$ km/h.

$$\frac{120 - 80}{80} \times 100\% = 50\%$$

Method 2: Writing Equations

We know $\text{speed} = \dfrac{\text{distance}}{\text{time}}$

$$\text{time} = \frac{\text{distance}}{\text{speed}}$$

$$\frac{d}{s} - \frac{d}{1.2 \times s} = 1 \qquad \text{.......................... (1)}$$

$$\frac{d}{s} - \frac{d}{p \times s} = 2 \qquad \text{.......................... (2)}$$

where p is the percentage increase in speed.

978-1-62399-075-6
Singapore Math Challenge

(1) × 2 − (2)

$$\frac{2f}{d} - \frac{2d}{1.2 \times s} - \frac{d}{s} + \frac{d}{p + s} = 0$$

$$\frac{d}{s} + \frac{d}{p \times s} - \frac{2d}{1.2 \times s} = 0 \qquad \text{.......................... (3)}$$

(3) × $\frac{s}{d}$

$$1 + \frac{1}{p} - \frac{5}{3} = 0$$

$$\frac{1}{p} - \frac{2}{3} = 0$$

$$\frac{1}{p} = \frac{2}{3}$$

$$p = 1.5$$

$$= 150\%$$

The speed should be increased by 50%.

978-1-62399-075-6
Singapore Math Challenge

1. In the number 3,141,592,653, compute the total number of appearances of digits 1, 3 and 5 in terms of percentage.

978-1-62399-075-6
Singapore Math Challenge

2. The bar graph shows the number of participants in a mathematics competition from the years 2006 to 2012. In which year is the increase sharpest in percentage terms?

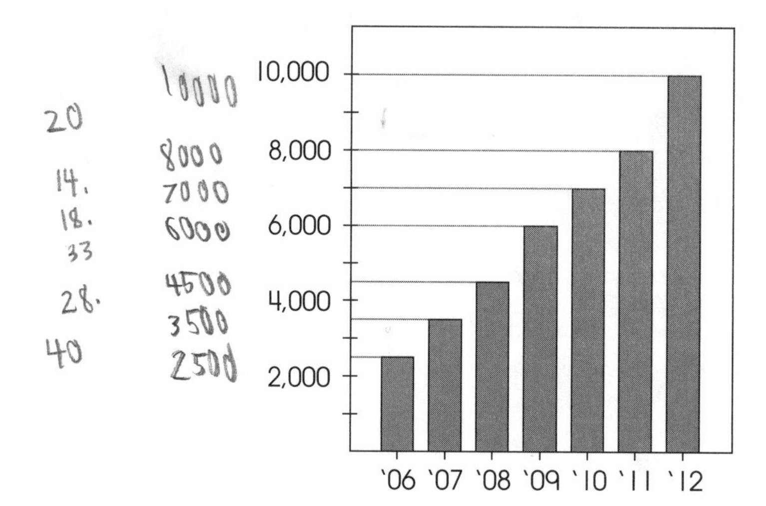

978-1-62399-075-6
Singapore Math Challenge

3. The side of a square is 10 cm. What is the increase in area in percentage if the side is lengthened by 3 cm?

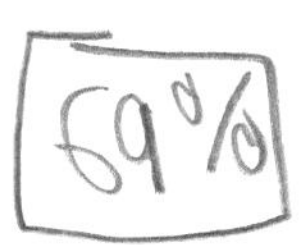

978-1-62399-075-6
Singapore Math Challenge

4. The volume of a cup of water increases by 10% when it turns to ice. By how much does the volume of ice decrease after it melts completely to water again? Give your answer in percentage.

1000

1100

$9\frac{1}{11}\%$

5. A company's sales volume increases by 20% in year 2. There is a further increase of 30% in year 3 compared to year 2. The sales in year 4, however, drop by 25% compared to year 3. What are the sales in year 4 compared to year 1? Express your answer in percentage.

100

120

156

156
− 39
117

6. A and B jointly set up a company in a 45%–55% partnership. The company makes a profit of $56,000 in the first year. How much of a share in dollars should A and B each get?

2800
x9
00

28000
2800
30800

28000
-2800
25200

A: 25200 B: 30800

7. Alice, Benny and Celine share $590. Alice has 20% more than Benny, and Celine has 25% less than Benny. How much more money does Alice have compared to Celine?

A
B
C

240
200
160

156
195

8. Adam's weekly pocket money is $80. On average, 20% goes to books and entertainment. He spends 3 times as much on food as he does on transportation. The money he saves is $6 less than his expenditure on food. What percent of his pocket money goes to savings?

80
64

24 80
6 20
30 100

30%

9. There are 2 containers of beads. Container A has 400 black beads and 250 white beads. Container B has 200 black beads and 670 white beads. How many black and white beads must be transferred from B to A so that 50% of the beads in A are white and 25% of the beads in B are black?

978-1-62399-075-6
Singapore Math Challenge

10. A sports shop imported some footballs and basketballs for $5,000. The selling price of a football is $40. The selling price of a basketball is 20% more than that of a football. There are 15 more basketballs than footballs. The total profit from the sales is $1,000. How many footballs are there?

978-1-62399-075-6
Singapore Math Challenge

11. The pie graph shows the population of an island.

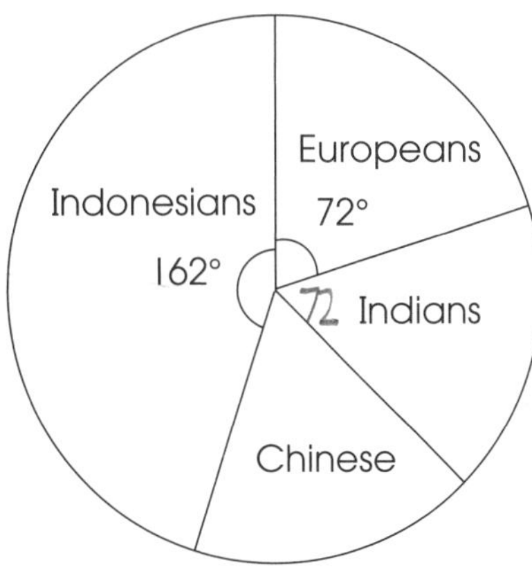

There are as many Indians as there are Europeans.
There are 100,000 more Indians than Chinese.
How many Indonesians are there on the island?

978-1-62399-075-6
Singapore Math Challenge

12. An elementary school had 2,000 students last year. This year, the number of boys increases by 20%, while the number of girls decreases by 20%. The total student population goes down by 4%. How many boys are there in the school this year?

2000

1920

13. Ethan has $40. He spends 20% of his money on soft drinks and snacks. He then buys 1,500 grams of apples at $6 per 500 grams. At the end, he needs to ask for a $2 discount on 1,000 grams of bananas so that his money is just enough. What is the discount on the bananas in percentage?

32
−18
14

978-1-62399-075-6
Singapore Math Challenge

14. In the first week, a shop bought some DVDs at $24 per pack of 4 DVDs. In the second week, it bought double the amount of DVDs at $25 per pack of 5 DVDs. The shop then repacked all the DVDs and sold them in packs of 3 DVDs. The profit gained was 20%. How much was each pack of 3 DVDs sold for?

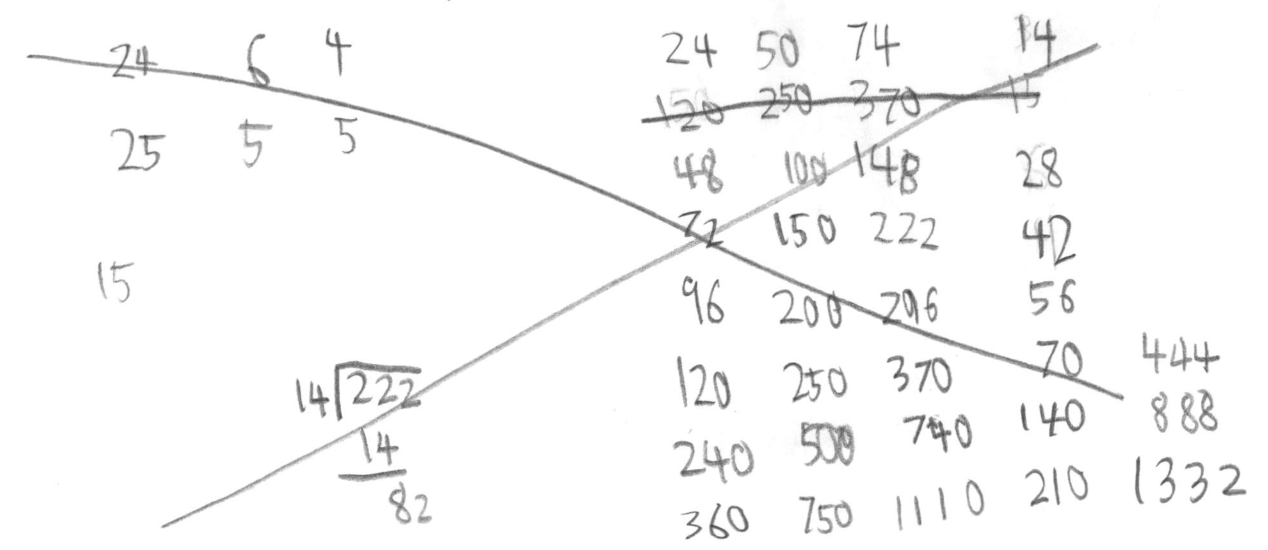

978-1-62399-075-6
Singapore Math Challenge

Angles and Triangles

Concept 1:

(a) Suppose l is a straight line, while l_1 and l_2 are two other straight lines that meet at a point on l.

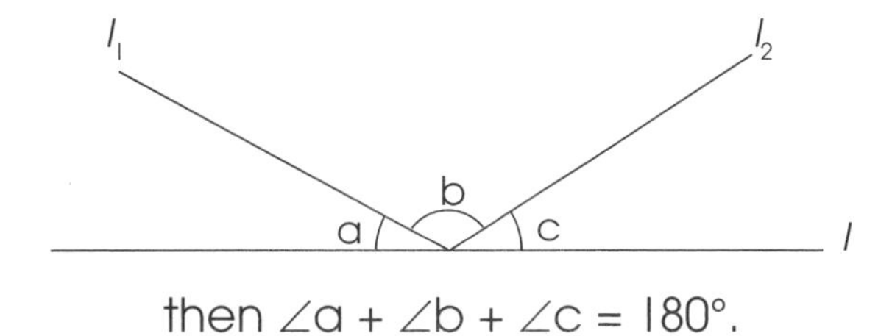

then $\angle a + \angle b + \angle c = 180°$.

(b) Given that l_1 and l_2 intersect at O.

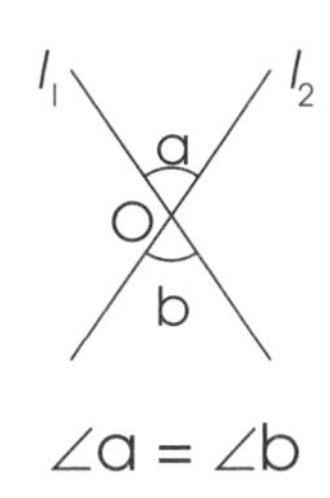

$\angle a = \angle b$

(c) If a point P on a line l travels one complete rotation around a fixed point O, it travels 360°.

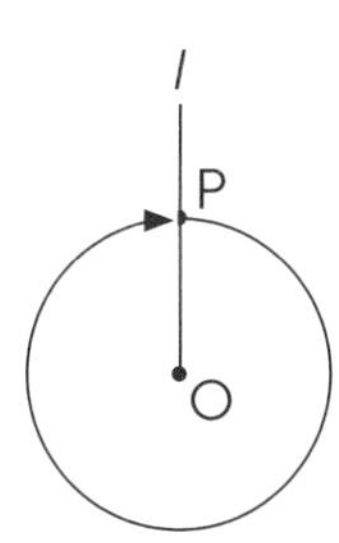

Concept 2: Given any triangle, the sum of its 3 interior angles is 180°.

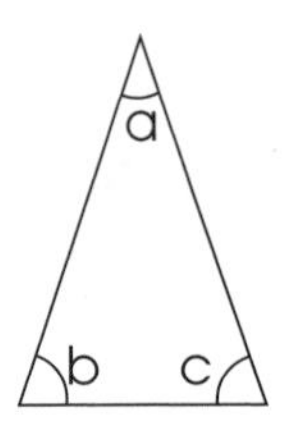

$$\angle a + \angle b + \angle c = 180°$$

Concept 3: Given a triangle, the exterior angle is the sum of its 2 opposite interior angles.

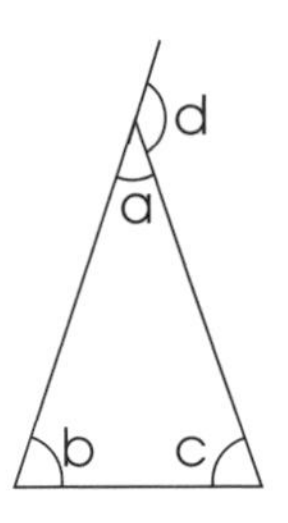

$$\angle d = \angle b + \angle c$$

By Concept 1(a), $\angle a = 180° - \angle d$
By Concept 2, $\angle a = 180° - (\angle b + \angle c)$
Equating, $180° - \angle d = 180° - (\angle b + \angle c)$
$\angle d = \angle b + \angle c$

978-1-62399-075-6

Concept 4: Given a right-angled triangle with sides a, b and c, where c is the longest side,

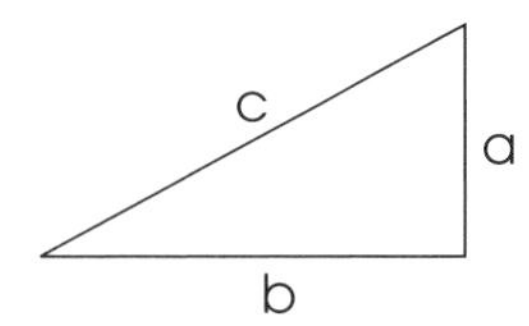

Pythagorean Triples are sets of 3 numbers that satisfy the Pythagorean Theorem.
Examples: (3, 4, 5), (5, 12, 13), (6, 8, 10), ...

The Pythagorean Theorem states that

$a^2 + b^2 = c^2$

Where a, b and c are whole numbers.

Concept 5: It may be interesting to observe that, for a quadrilateral, the sum of its 4 interior angles is $2 \times 180° = 360°$.

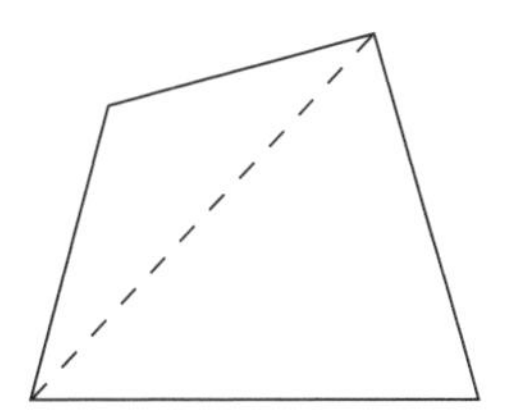

This is so a dotted line can be drawn to separate it into 2 triangles.

978-1-62399-075-6

Concept 6: For a parallelogram, for which there are 2 pairs of parallel sides,

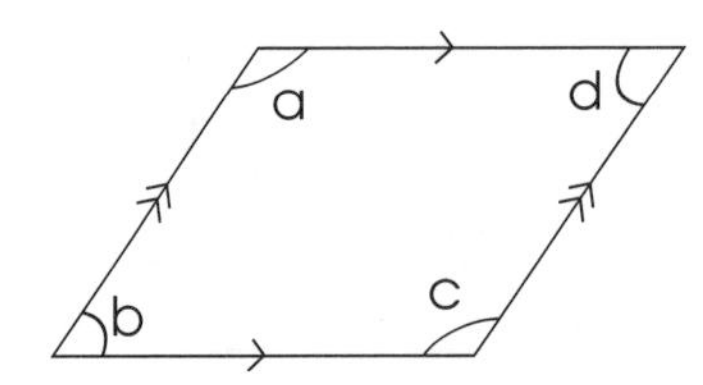

we say that $\angle a + \angle b = 180°$ or $\angle a + \angle d = 180°$
$\angle c + \angle d = 180°$ $\angle a + \angle d = 180°$

For an isosceles trapezoid, there are a pair of parallel sides and 2 identical sides.

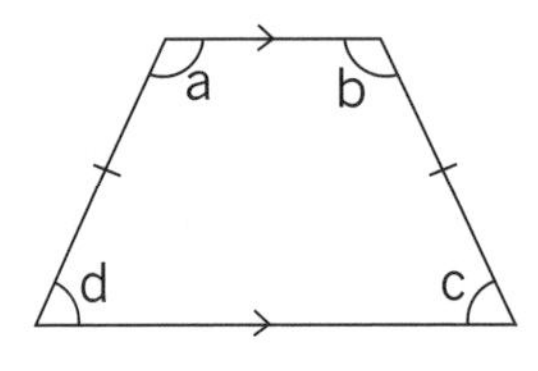

$\angle a + \angle d = 180°$
$\angle b + \angle c = 180°$
$\angle a = \angle b$
$\angle c = \angle d$

978-1-62399-075-6
Singapore Math Challenge

Example 1: 3 lines intersect one another to form a triangle. Find ∠d.

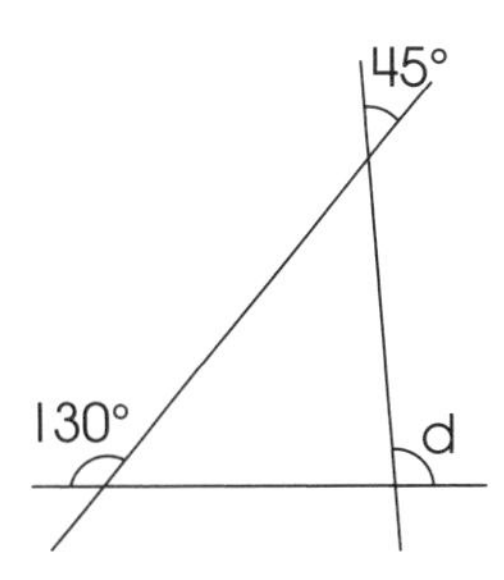

Solution:

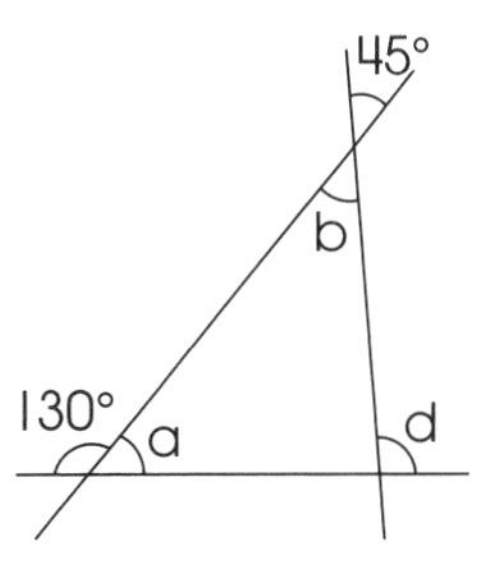

$\angle a = 180° - 130°$
$= 50°$

$\angle b = 45°$

$\angle d = \angle a + \angle b$
$= 50° + 45°$
$= 95°$

978-1-62399-075-6
Singapore Math Challenge

Example 2: A rectangular piece of paper is folded, as shown.
Find $\angle a$.

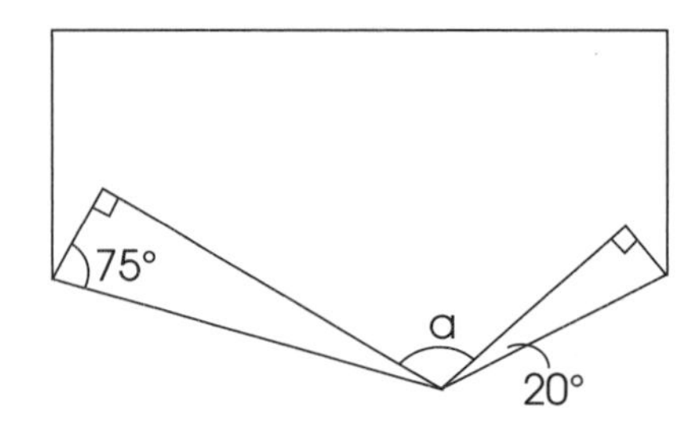

Solution:

$\angle b = 180° - 90° - 75°$
$= 15°$

$\angle c = \angle b = 15°$
Likewise, $\angle d = 20°$.

$\angle a = 180° - 2 \times 15° - 2 \times 20°$
$= 180° - 30° - 40°$
$= 110°$

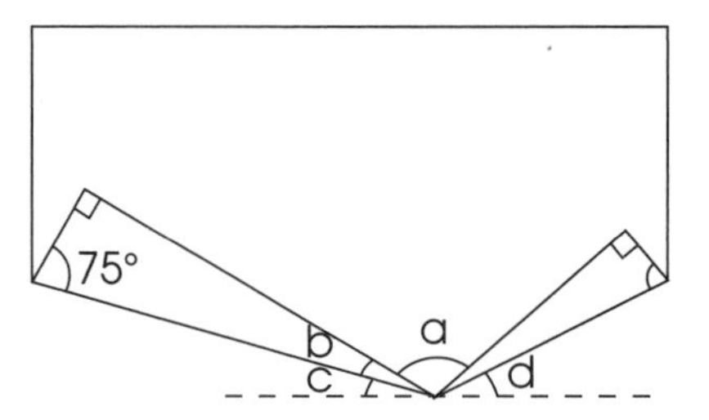

978-1-62399-075-6
Singapore Math Challenge

Example 3: ABCD is a square. ∠BPC is an equilateral triangle.
AB = BP and CD = CP. Find ∠ADP.

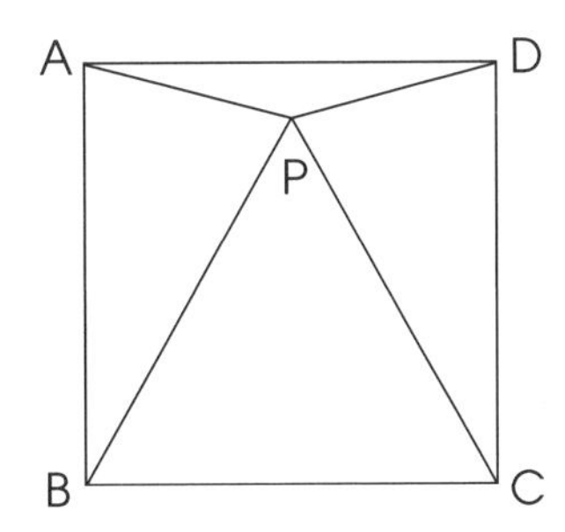

Solution:

For an equilateral triangle, each interior angle

$= \frac{180°}{3} = 60°$

It follows that

∠DCP = ∠ABP = 90° − 60°
= 30°

∠CDP = ∠CPD
= (180° − 30°) ÷ 2
= 75°

∠ADP = 90° − 75°
= 15°

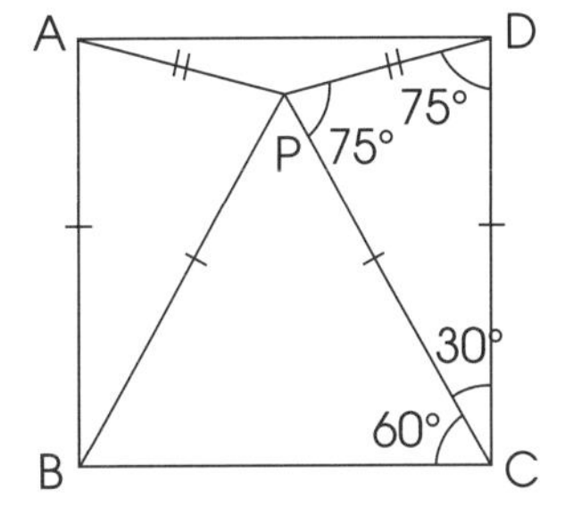

978-1-62399-075-6
Singapore Math Challenge

Example 4: In the diagram, BE = AC, $\angle CAE = 30°$ and $\angle AEB = 70°$. Find $\angle ABC$.

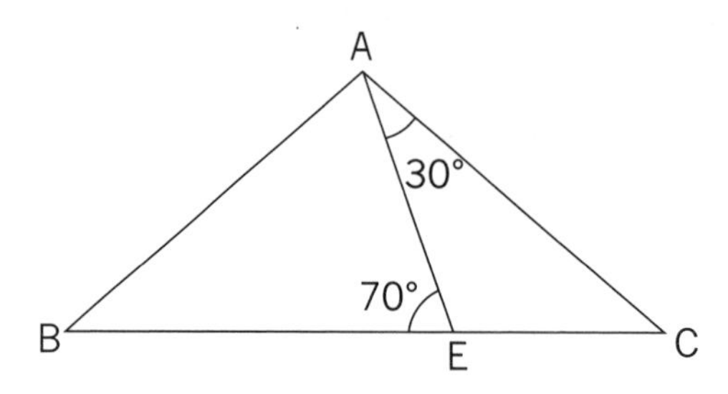

Solution:

Since BE = AC, we can cut along AE and paste AC along BE.

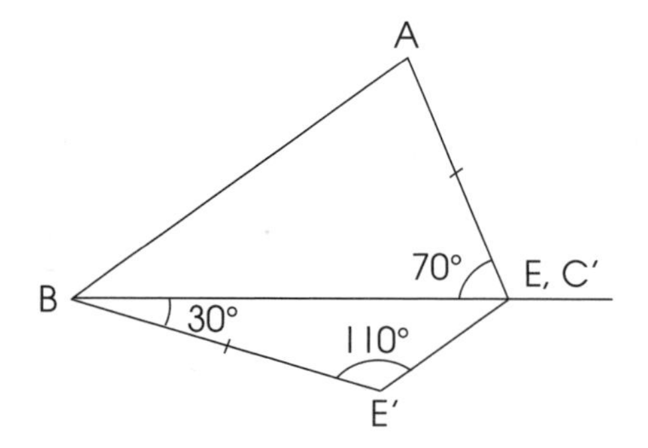

The figure then becomes an isosceles trapezoid.
In the original figure, $\angle AEC = 110°$.
Therefore, $\angle BE'C' = 110°$.

$\angle BC'E' = 180° - 30° - 110° = 40°$

$\angle ABE' = \dfrac{360° - 110° - 110°}{2} = 70°$

$\angle ABC = 70° - 30° = 40°$

Example 5: It is given that $\angle BAC = 108°$.
AD bisects $\angle BAC$ and AB + BD = AC.
Find $\angle C$.

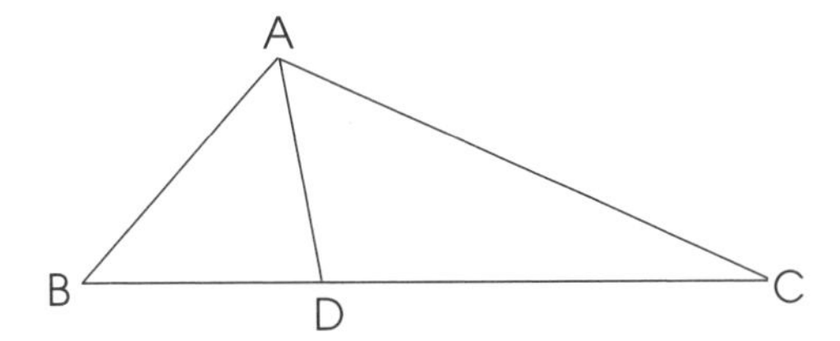

Solution:

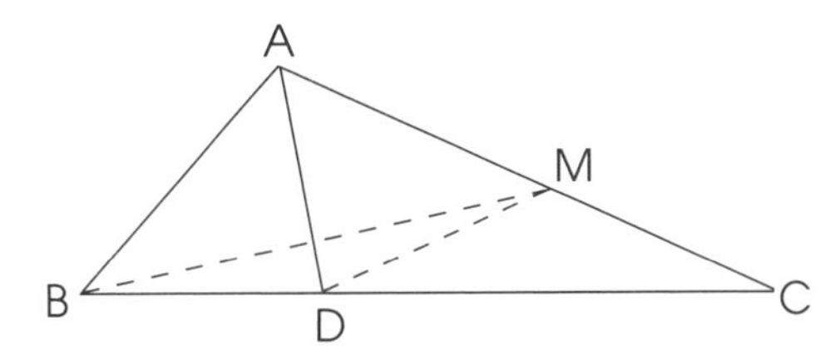

Let M be the midpoint of AC.
Then AB = AM, since AD bisects $\angle BAC$.
$\angle ABD$ is identical to $\angle ADM$.

BD = DM = CM

$\angle C = \angle CDM$

$= \frac{1}{2} \angle AMD$ (exterior angle)

$= \frac{1}{2} \angle B$

$\angle B + \angle C = 180° - 108°$

$= 72°$

$\angle C = 24°$

978-1-62399-075-6
Singapore Math Challenge

1. A regular pentagon has 5 equal sides. Show that each interior angle is 108°.

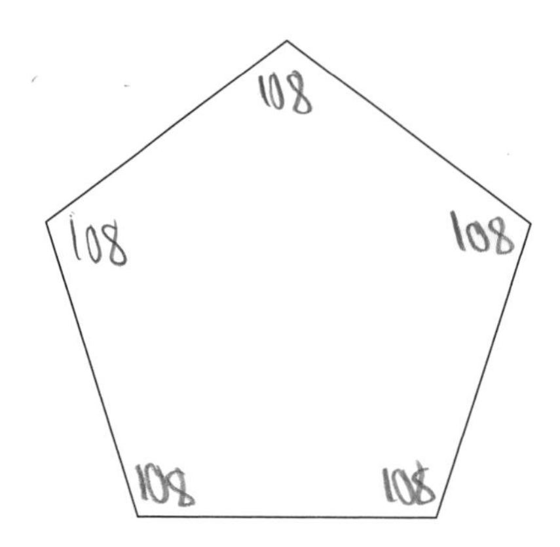

5 - 2 = 3

180 x 3 = 540

978-1-62399-075-6

2. In the diagram below, AB = AC = AD, ∠ABC = 40° and ∠ACD = 80°. Find ∠BAD.

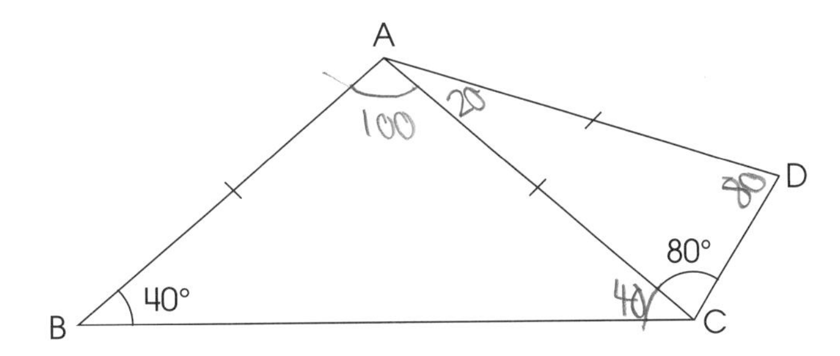

978-1-62399-075-6
Singapore Math Challenge

 Name ____________________ Date ____________

3. Find ∠A + ∠B + ∠C + ∠D.

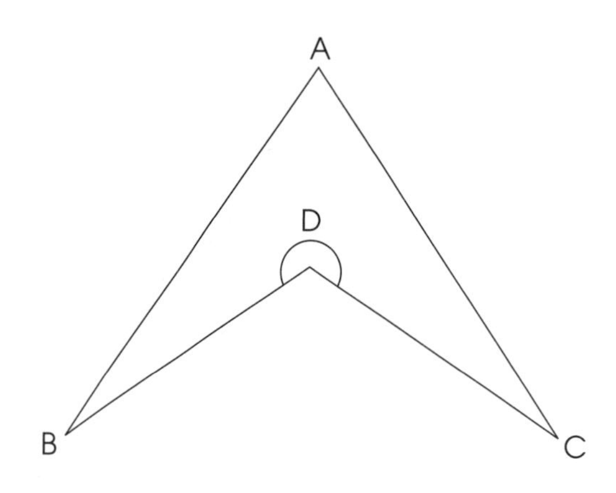

978-1-62399-075-6
Singapore Math Challenge

4. ABCD is a square and Δ BCE is equilateral. Find $\angle$AED.

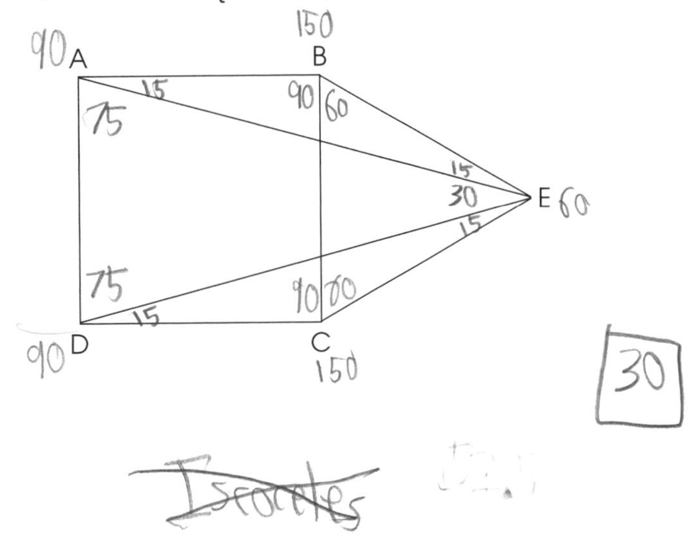

5. Find ∠a + ∠b + ∠c + ∠d + ∠e + ∠f.

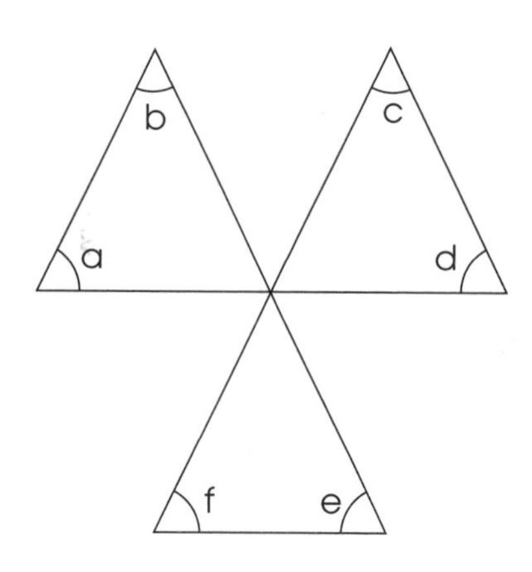

978-1-62399-075-6

6. The perimeter of a right-angled triangle is 30 cm. Its area is 30 cm^2. Find its longest side.

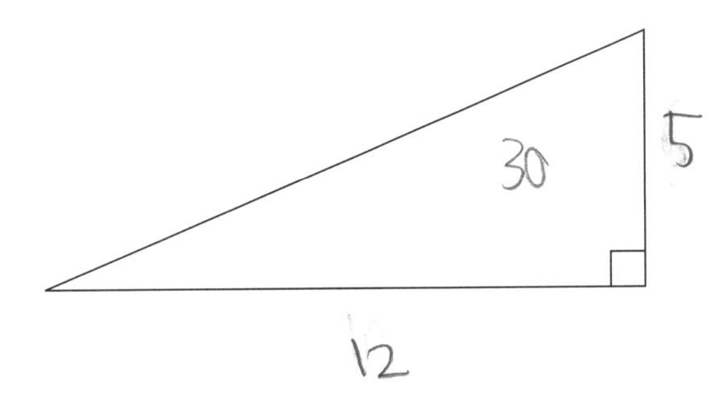

60

978-1-62399-075-6
Singapore Math Challenge

7. In ΔABC, $\angle B = 90°$, DE is perpendicular to AC and divides it into 2 equal lengths. Ratio of $\angle DCE : \angle BCE = 5 : 2$. Find $\angle ACB$.

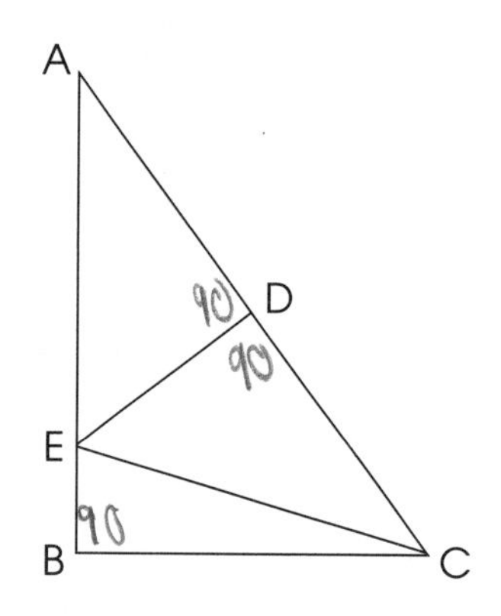

52.5

8. In $\triangle ABC$, $AB = AC$, $AD = AE$ and $\angle BAD = 60°$. Find $\angle CDE$.

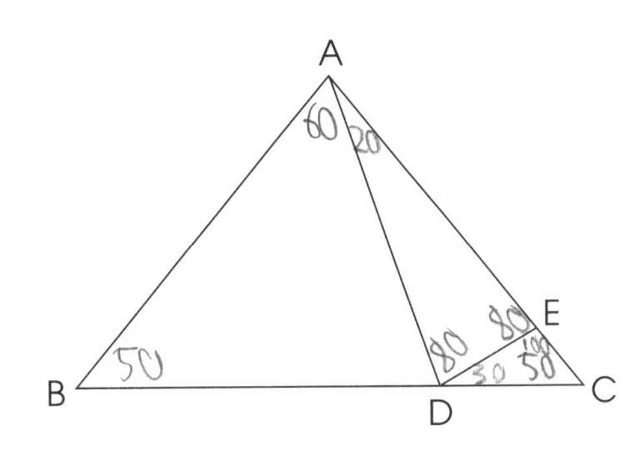

9. In ΔABC, $\angle BAC = 45°$ and M is the intersection of heights BD and CD. Find $\angle BMC$.

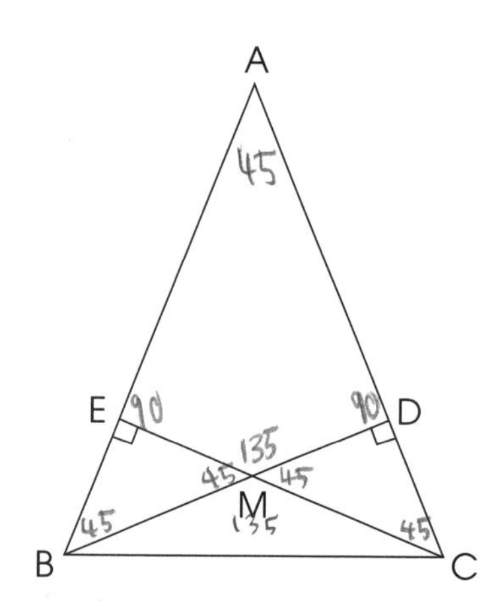

978-1-62399-075-6

10. ABCD is a quadrilateral. AB = BC = CD, ∠ACB + ∠CAD = 180° and ∠D = 40°. Find ∠ACD.

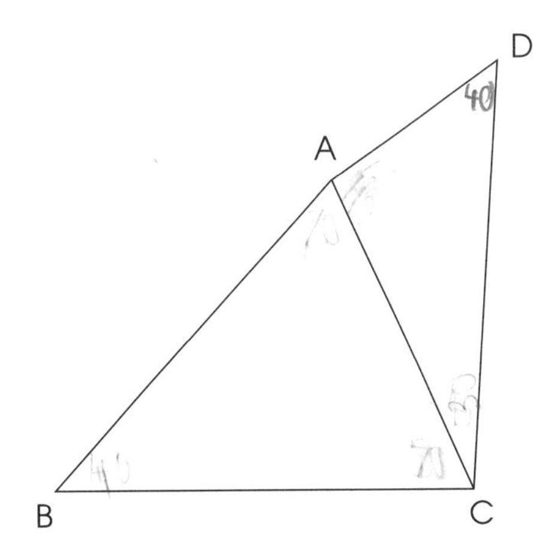

 Name ______________________ Date __________

11. $\triangle ABC$ and $\triangle CDE$ are both right-angled triangles. Their heights are AB and DE respectively and they intersect at P. Given that $\angle BPE = 50°$, find $\angle C$.

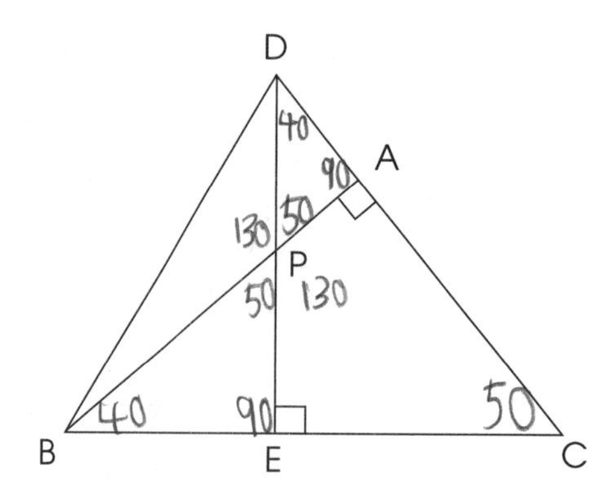

978-1-62399-075-6

12. The sum of 3 exterior angles of a triangle is 360°. The ratio of these angles is 2 : 3 : 4. Find the ratio of the 3 interior angles.

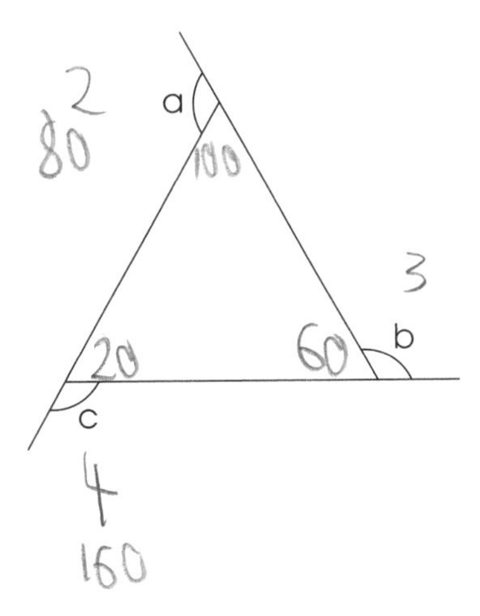

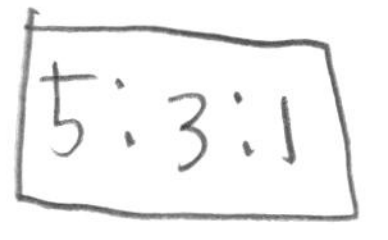

80 120 160

13. In ΔABC, $\angle B = 80°$, AD = AE and CD = CF. Find $\angle EDF$.

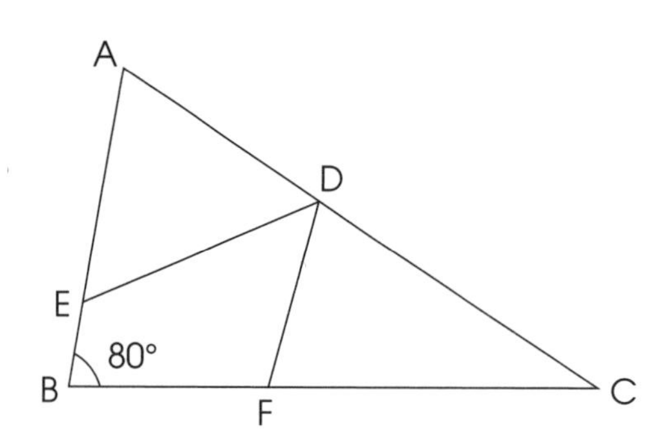

14. In △ABC, AB = AC, AE = DE = CD and BC = CE. Find ∠A.

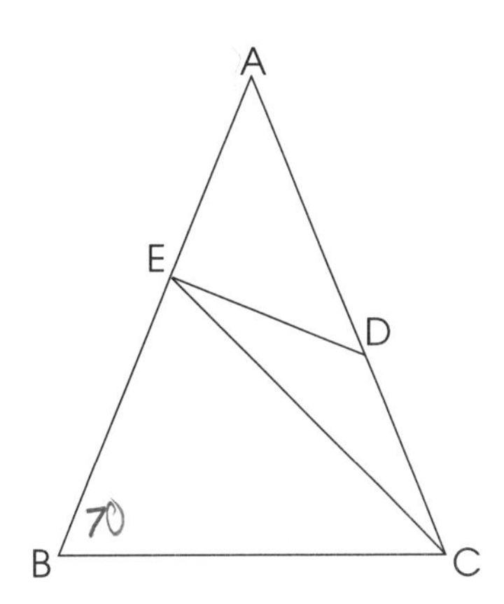

978-1-62399-075-6
Singapore Math Challenge

Solutions

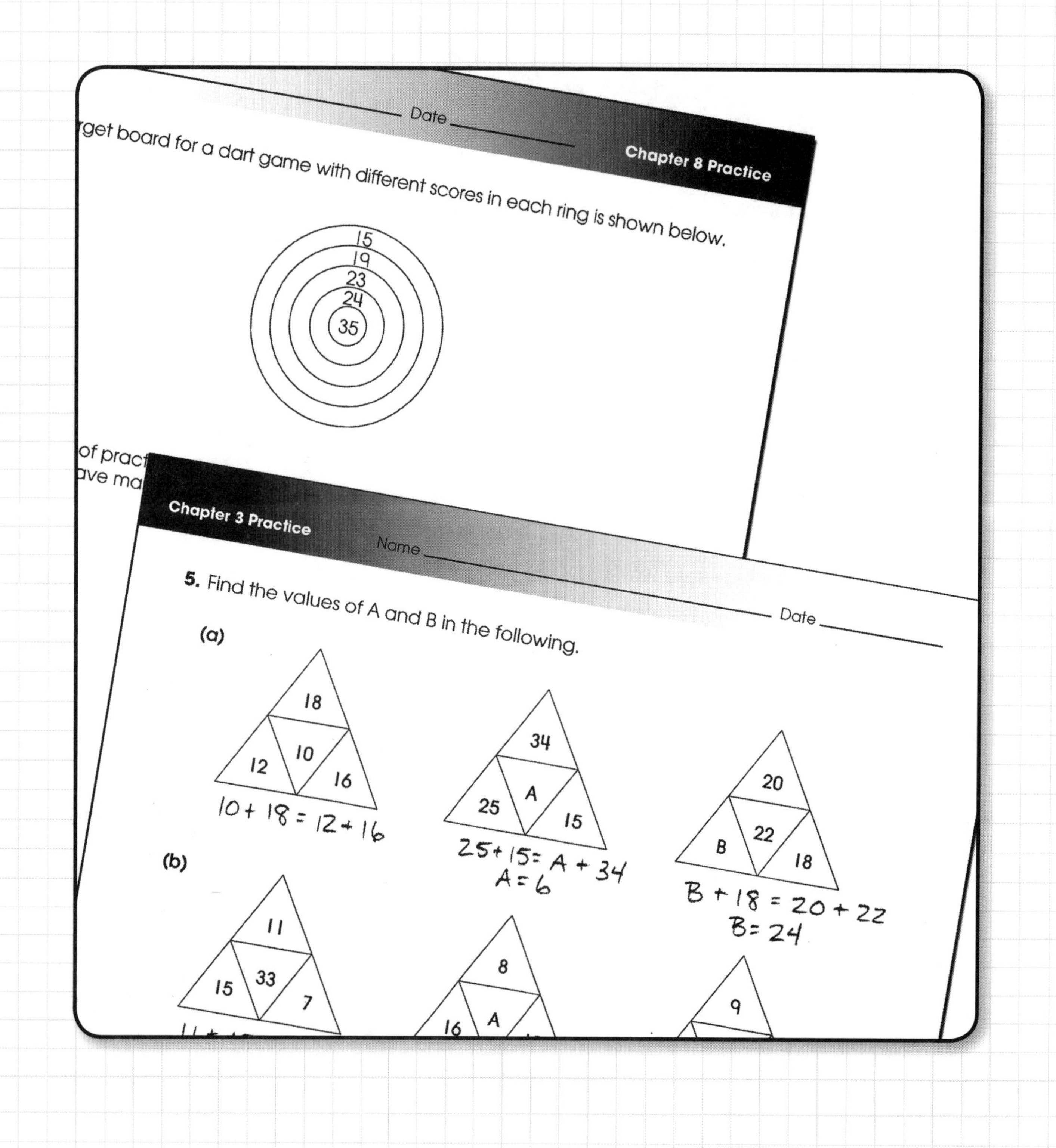

Date
get board for a dart game with different scores in each ring is shown below.
Chapter 8 Practice
15
19
23
24
35
of pract
ave ma
Chapter 3 Practice
Name
Date
5. Find the values of A and B in the following.
(a)
18
12
10
16
10 + 18 = 12 + 16
34
25
A
15
25 + 15 = A + 34
A = 6
20
B
22
18
B + 18 = 20 + 22
B = 24
(b)
11
15
33
7
8
16
A
9

Chapter 1 Practice

Page 13

1. (a) $456 + 88 - 56$
$= 400 + 88$
$= 488$

(b) $374 + 56 - 74$
$= 300 + 56$
$= 356$

(c) $3,035 - 998 - 997$
$= 3,035 - 1,000 + 2 - 1,000 + 3$
$= 1,035 + 5$
$= 1,040$

(d) $999 + 3 + 98 + 998 + 3 + 9$
$= 999 + 1 + 2 + 98 + 998 + 2 + 1 + 9$
$= 1,000 + 100 + 1,000 + 10$
$= 2,110$

(e) $636 - 567 - 99 + 367$
$= 536 + 100 - 99 - 567 + 367$
$= 536 + 1 - 200$
$= 337$

(f) $5,034 - 997 - 998 - 999$
$= 5,034 - 3,000 + 6$
$= 2,034 + 6$
$= 2,040$

(g) $\overbrace{123 + \underbrace{456 + 544}_{1,000} + 877}^{1,000}$
$= 1,000 + 1,000$
$= 2,000$

(h) $\underbrace{3,456 + \overbrace{4,567 + 6,544}_{}}_{10,000} + 5,433$ (4,567 + 5,433 = 10,000; 3,456 + 6,544 = 10,000)
$= 10,000 + 10,000$
$= 20,000$

Page 14, 15

2. (a) $2,208 - (208 + 139)$
$= 2,208 - 208 - 139$
$= 2,000 - 139$
$= 1,861$

(b) $733 - (33 + 320) = 733 - 33 - 320$
$= 700 - 320$
$= 380$

(c) $1,306 - (406 - 258)$
$= 1,306 - 406 + 258$
$= 900 + 258$
$= 1,158$

(d) $945 + (372 - 245) - 172$
$= 945 + 372 - 245 - 172$ (372 − 172 = 200; 945 − 245 = 700)
$= 700 + 200$
$= 900$

(e) $644 - (243 - 156) + 143$
$= 644 - 243 + 156 + 143$
$= 644 + 156 - 243 + 143$
$= 800 - 100$
$= 700$

(f) $717 - (617 - 225)$
$= 717 - 617 + 225$
$= 100 + 225$
$= 325$

(g) $937 - (137 + 185) + 85$
$= 937 - 137 - 185 + 85$
$= 800 - 100$
$= 700$

(h) $1,732 - (732 - 257)$
$= 1,732 - 732 + 257$
$= 1,000 + 257$
$= 1,257$

(i) $788 - (288 + 546) + 346$
$= \underbrace{788 - 288}_{500} - \underbrace{546 + 346}_{200}$
$= 500 - 200$
$= 300$

978-1-62399-075-6

Page 16

3. (a) 37 + 397 + 3,997 + 39,997
= 40 + 400 + 4,000 + 40,000 − 4 × 3
= 44,440 − 12
= 44,428

(b) 298 + 2,998 + 29,998 + 299,998
= 300 + 3,000 + 30,000 + 300,000 − 4 × 2
= 333,300 − 8
= 333,292

(c) 9 + 99 + 999 + 9,999 + 99,999
= 10 + 100 + 1,000 + 10,000 + 100,000 − 5
= 111,110 − 5
= 111,105

Page 17

4.

(a) (2 + 4 + 6 + ... + 2,006) − (1 + 3 + 5 + ... + 2,005) [difference: 1]
= 1,003 × 1
= 1,003

(b) 88 − 87 + 86 − 85 + ... + 4 − 3 + 2 − 1 [each pair: 1]
= 44 × 1
= 44

(c) 100 − 98 + 96 − 94 + ... + 8 − 6 + 4 − 2 [each pair: 2; step: 4]
100 − 4 = 96
96 ÷ 4 = 24
24 + 1 = 25 pairs of twos
25 × 2 = 50

Page 18

5. (a) 360 − 357 + 354 − 351 + ... + 300 − 297 [each pair: 3; step: 6]
360 − 300 = 60
60 ÷ 6 + 1 = 11 pairs of threes
11 × 3 = 33

(b) 2,006 − 1 − 2 − 3 − 4 − ... − 48 − 49 − 50
= 2,006 − (1 + 2 + 3 + ... + 49 + 50)
= 2,006 − (51 × 25)
= 2,006 − 1,275
= 731

(c) 280 − 276 + 272 − 268 + ... + 200 − 196 [each pair: 4; step: 8]
280 − 200 = 80
80 ÷ 8 + 1 = 11 pairs of fours
11 × 4 = 44

978-1-62399-075-6
Singapore Math Challenge

Page 19, 20

6. (a) $56 \times 8 + 88 \times 4$
$= 56 \times 2 \times 4 + 88 \times 4$
$= 4 \times (112 + 88)$
$= 4 \times 200$
$= 800$

(b) $1{,}600 \div 25$
$= 16 \times 100 \div 25$
$= 16 \times 4$
$= 64$

(c) $56 \times 33 + 44 \times 33$
$= (56 + 44) \times 33$
$= 100 \times 33$
$= 3{,}300$

(d) $73 \times 12 + 27 \times 12$
$= (73 + 27) \times 12$
$= 100 \times 12$
$= 1{,}200$

(e) 198×56
$= (200 - 2) \times 56$
$= 11{,}200 - 112$
$= 11{,}088$

(f) $5 \times 64 \times 25 \times 125 \times 97$
$= 5 \times 8 \times 8 \times 25 \times 125 \times 97$
10 100 1,000
$= 5 \times 2 \times 4 \times 8 \times 25 \times 125 \times 97$
$= 1{,}000{,}000 \times 97$
$= 97{,}000{,}000$

(g) $64 \times 25 \times 125 \times 16$
100 1,000
$= 2 \times 4 \times 8 \times 25 \times 125 \times 16$
$= 32 \times 100{,}000$
$= 3{,}200{,}000$

(h) $16{,}000 \div 25$
$= 160 \times 100 \div 25$
$= 160 \times 4$
$= 640$

(i) $125 \times 25 \times 5 \times 64$
$= 125 \times 25 \times 5 \times 2 \times 4 \times 8$
$= 1{,}000 \times 100 \times 10$
$= 1{,}000{,}000$

(j) $101 \times 1{,}001 - 101$
$= 101 \times (1{,}001 - 1)$
$= 101 \times 1{,}000$
$= 101{,}000$

Page 20, 21

7. (a) $5{,}000 \div 8 \div 125$
$= 5{,}000 \div (8 \times 125)$
$= 5{,}000 \div 1{,}000$
$= 5$

(b) $6{,}000 \div 25 \div 4$
$= 6{,}000 \div (25 \times 4)$
$= 6{,}000 \div 100$
$= 60$

10 1,000
(c) $30{,}000 \div 2 \div 8 \div 5 \div 125$
$= 30{,}000 \div 10 \div 1{,}000$
$= 3$

1,000
(d) $16{,}000 \div 125 \div 4 \div 8$
$= 16{,}000 \div 1{,}000 \div 4$
$= 16 \div 4$
$= 4$

(e) $32{,}000 \div 125$
$= 32 \times 1{,}000 \div 125$
$= 32 \times 8$
$= 256$

(f) $5{,}300 \div 25$
$= 53 \times 100 \div 25$
$= 53 \times 4$
$= 212$

(g) $1{,}400 \div 25$
$= 14 \times 100 \div 25$
$= 14 \times 4$
$= 56$

(h) $72{,}000 \div 125$
$= 72 \times 1{,}000 \div 125$
$= 72 \times 8$
$= 576$

978-1-62399-075-6
Singapore Math Challenge

Page 21, 22

8. (a) $89 \times 11 + 11 \times 11$
$= (89 + 11) \times 11$
$= 100 \times 11$
$= 1,100$

(b) $29 \times 8 + 42 \times 4$
$= 29 \times 2 \times 4 + 42 \times 4$
$= 58 \times 4 + 42 \times 4$
$= (58 + 42) \times 4$
$= 100 \times 4$
$= 400$

(c) $58 \times 8 + 84 \times 4$
$= 58 \times 2 \times 4 + 84 \times 4$
$= 116 \times 4 + 84 \times 4$
$= (116 + 84) \times 4$
$= 200 \times 4$
$= 800$

(d) $58 \times 30 + 84 \times 15$
$= 58 \times 2 \times 15 + 84 \times 15$
$= 116 \times 15 + 84 \times 15$
$= 200 \times 15$
$= 3,000$

(e) $63 \times 6 + 74 \times 3$
$= 63 \times 2 \times 3 + 74 \times 3$
$= 126 \times 3 + 74 \times 3$
$= (126 + 74) \times 3$
$= 200 \times 3$
$= 600$

(f) $74 \times 6 + 152 \times 3$
$= 74 \times 2 \times 3 + 152 \times 3$
$= 148 \times 3 + 152 \times 3$
$= (148 + 152) \times 3$
$= 300 \times 3$
$= 900$

(g) $44 \times 4 + 78 \times 8$
$= 22 \times 2 \times 4 + 78 \times 8$
$= 22 \times 8 + 78 \times 8$
$= (22 + 78) \times 8$
$= 100 \times 8$
$= 800$

(h) $56 \times 16 + 72 \times 32$
$= 28 \times 2 \times 16 + 72 \times 32$
$= (28 + 72) \times 32$
$= 3,200$

Page 23

9. (a) $35 \times 128 - 28 \times 35$
$= 35 \times (128 - 28)$
$= 35 \times 100$
$= 3,500$

(b) $46 \times 234 - 134 \times 46$
$= 46 \times (234 - 134)$
$= 46 \times 100$
$= 4,600$

(c) $287 \times 12 - 187 \times 12$
$= (287 - 187) \times 12$
$= 100 \times 12$
$= 1,200$

(d) $897 \times 30 - 297 \times 30$
$= (897 - 297) \times 30$
$= 600 \times 30$
$= 18,000$

(e) $69 \times 36 - 38 \times 18$
$= 69 \times 2 \times 18 - 38 \times 18$
$= 138 \times 18 - 38 \times 18$
$= (138 - 38) \times 18$
$= 100 \times 18$
$= 1,800$

(f) $74 \times 54 - 48 \times 27$
$= 74 \times 2 \times 27 - 48 \times 27$
$= 148 \times 27 - 48 \times 27$
$= (148 - 48) \times 27$
$= 100 \times 27$
$= 2,700$

(g) $132 \times 36 - 196 \times 12$
$= 132 \times 3 \times 12 - 196 \times 12$
$= 396 \times 12 - 196 \times 12$
$= (396 - 196) \times 12$
$= 200 \times 12$
$= 2,400$

(h) $156 \times 48 - 124 \times 12$
$= 156 \times 4 \times 12 - 124 \times 12$
$= 624 \times 12 - 124 \times 12$
$= (624 - 124) \times 12$
$= 500 \times 12$
$= 6,000$

Page 24

10. (a) $3,333 \times 3,333 \div 9,999$
$= 3,333 \times 3 \times 1,111 \div 9,999$
$= 9,999 \times 1,111 \div 9,999$
$= 1,111$

(b) $2,222 \times 9,999 \div 3,333$
$= 2,222 \times 3 \times 3,333 \div 3,333$
$= 6,666$

(c) $99,999 \times 88,888 \div 11,111$
$= 99,999 \times 8 \times 11,111 \div 11,111$
$= 799,992$

(d) $6,666 \times 8 + 4,444 \times 13$
$= 1,111 \times 6 \times 8 + 1,111 \times 4 \times 13$
$= 1,111 \times 48 + 1,111 \times 52$
$= 1,111 \times (48 + 52)$
$= 111,100$

Chapter 2 Practice

Page 30

1. If all are rabbits, there will be $45 \times 4 = 180$ legs.
$180 - 140 = 40$
$4 - 2 = 2$
$40 \div 2 = 20$ chickens
$45 - 20 = 25$ rabbits
The farmer has 20 chickens and 25 rabbits.

2. If all are spiders, there will be $28 \times 8 = 224$ legs.
$224 - 200 = 24$
$8 - 6 = 2$
$24 \div 2 = 12$ dragonflies
$28 - 12 = 16$ spiders
There are 16 spiders and 12 dragonflies.

Page 31

3. If all were five-dollar toys, he would have spent \$20 × \$5 = \$100.
\$100 - \$55 = \$45
\$5 - \$2 = \$3
\$45 ÷ \$3 = 15 two-dollar toys
20 - 15 = 5 five-dollar toys
He bought 15 two-dollar toys and 5 five-dollar toys.

4. If all are cars, there will be $40 \times 4 = 160$ wheels.
$160 - 116 = 44$
$4 - 2 = 2$
$44 \div 2 = 22$ motorcycles
$40 - 22 = 18$ cars
There are 18 cars and 22 motorcycles.

978-1-62399-075-6
Singapore Math Challenge

Page 32

5. If all were adult tickets, he would have paid
$20 \times \$35 = \$700$.
$\$700 - \$598 = \$102$
$\$35 - \$18 = \$17$
$\$102 \div \$17 = 6$ food tickets
$20 - 6 = 14$ adult tickets
He bought 14 adult tickets and 6 food tickets.

6. If all are ten-dollar bills, he will have
$20 \times \$10 = \$200$.
$\$200 - \$125 = \$75$
$\$10 - \$5 = \$5$
$\$75 \div \$5 = 15$ five-dollar bills
$20 - 15 = 5$ ten-dollar bills
He has 15 five-dollar bills and 5 ten-dollar bills.

Page 33

7. If Kelly answers all questions correctly, she will get $15 \times 2 = 30$ points.
$30 - 21 = 9$ points
The difference in points between a correct answer and a wrong answer is $2 + 1 = 3$ points.
$9 \div 3 = 3$ wrong answers
$15 - 3 = 12$ correct answers
She answers 12 questions correctly.

8. If Rena gets all questions correct, she will score $30 \times 5 = 150$ points.
$150 - 126 = 24$
$5 + 3 = 8$
$24 \div 8 = 3$ wrong answers
She gets 3 questions wrong.

Page 34

9. Full points for the quiz $= 20 \times 4 + 10 \times 7$
$= 150$
$150 - 124 = 26$
$3 \times 4 + 2 \times 7 = 26$
He answers 3 of the first 20 questions and 2 of the last 10 questions incorrectly.

10. ***Method 1***
If all were chairs,
$\$375 - 5 \times \$20 = \$275$
$5 + 6 = 11$ chairs
$\$275 \div 11 = \$25$ for each chair
$\$25 + \$20 = \$45$ for each table
Method 2
If all were tables,
$\$375 + 6 \times \$20 = \$495$
$5 + 6 = 11$ tables
$\$495 \div 11 = \$45$ for each table
$\$45 - \$20 = \$25$ for each chair
The prices of a table and a chair were \$45 and \$25 respectively.

Page 35

11. ***Method 1***
If all were volleyballs,
$\$390 - 5 \times \$15 = \$315$
$5 + 4 = 9$
$\$315 \div 9 = \$35$ for a volleyball
$\$35 + \$15 = \$50$ for a basketball
Method 2
If all were basketballs,
$\$390 + 4 \times \$15 = \$450$
$5 + 4 = 9$
$\$450 \div 9 = \$50$ for a basketball
$\$50 - \$15 = \$35$ for a volleyball
The prices of a basketball and a volleyball were \$50 and \$35 respectively.

12. We "create" a new denomination.
$(\$10 + \$2) \div 2 = \$6$ bill
Method 1
If all are \$6 bills, $20 \times \$6 = \$120$.
$\$120 - \$110 = \$10$
$\$6 - \$5 = \$1$
$10 \div \$1 = 10$ \$5 bills
$(20 - 10) \div 2 = 5$ \$2 bills
and 5 \$10 bills
Method 2
If all are \$5 bills, $20 \times \$5 = \$100$.
$\$110 - \$100 = \$10$
$\$6 - \$5 = \$1$
$10 \div \$1 = 10$ \$6 bills
$20 - 10 = 10$ \$5 bills
He has 5 \$2 bills, 10 \$5 bills and 5 \$10 bills.

978-1-62399-075-6
Singapore Math Challenge

Chapter 3 Practice

Page 36

1.

(a) 1, 2, 4, 8, 16, 32, 64, ...
(×2 ×2 ×2 ×2 ×2 ×2)

(b) 3, 4, 5, 8, 7, 16, 9, 32, 11, 64, ...
(×2 ×2 ×2 ×2; +2 +2 +2 +2)

(c) 0, 3, 8, 15, 24, 35, 48, 63, ...
(+3 +5 +7 +9 +11 +13 +15)

(d) 6, 1, 8, 3, 10, 5, 12, 7, 14, 9, ...
(+2 +2 +2 +2; +2 +2 +2 +2)

(e) 2, 3, 5, 8, 12, 17, 23, ...
(+1 +2 +3 +4 +5 +6)

(f) 3, 5, 6, 10, 9, 15, 12, 20, ...
(+5 +5 +5; +3 +3 +3)

(g) 7, 11, 19, 35, 67, 131, 259, ...
(+4 +8 +16 +32 +64 +128)

(h) 8, 12, 20, 32, 52, 84, ...
(+4 +8 +12 +20 +32)

Page 37

2. **(a)** $8 \times 2 + 4 = 20$
$18 \times 2 + 4 = 40$
$33 \times 2 + 4 = 70$

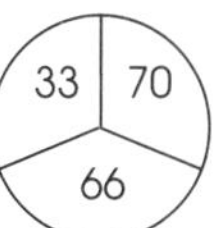

(b) $3 \times 7 = 21$
$21 + 3 = 24$

$9 \times 7 = 63$
$63 + 3 = 66$

$10 \times 7 = 70$
$70 + 3 = 73$

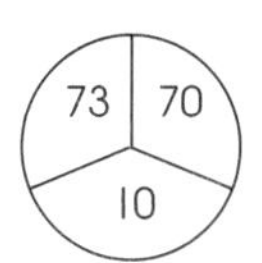

(c) $34 - 3 = 31$
$31 - 5 = 26$

$42 - 3 = 39$
$39 - 5 = 35$

$55 - 3 = 52$
$52 - 5 = 47$

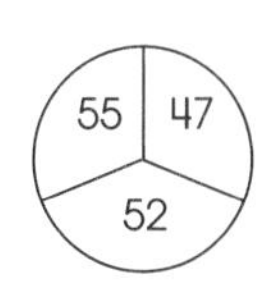

Page 38

3. 1,234 × 9 + 5 = 11,111
12,345 × 9 + 6 = 111,111
1,234,567 × 9 + 8 = 11,111,111

4. 1, 5, 14, 30, 55, 91, 140, 204, ⋯
(differences: +4, +9, +16, +25, +36, +49, +64)

Page 39

5. **(a)** 10 + 18 = 12 + 16
25 + 15 = A + 34   A = 6
B + 18 = 20 + 22   B = 24

(b) 11 + 15 + 7 = 33
8 + 16 + 10 = A   A = 34
9 + 14 + 12 = B   B = 35

(c) 3 × 4 × 5 ÷ 2 = A   A = 30
8 × 3 × 1 ÷ 2 = 12
2 × 3 × 5 ÷ 2 = 15

Page 40

6. 11,111 × 11,111 = 123,454,321
111,111 × 111,111 = 12,345,654,321
1,111,111 × 1,111,111 = 1,234,567,654,321
11,111,111 × 11,111,111 = 123,456,787,654,321

7. 8,547 × 78 = 666,666
8,547 × 104 = 888,888
8,547 × 117 = 999,999
8,547 × 65 = 555,555

Page 41

8. **(a)** 2, 3, 5, 8, 13, 21, 34, 55, ⋯
(differences: +2, +3, +5, +8, +13, +21)

(b) 1, 4, 9, 16, 25, 36, 49, ⋯

(c) 6, 3, 8, 5, 10, 7, 12, 9, ⋯
(+2, +2, +2 above; +2, +2, +2 below)

(d) 9, 11, 15, 21, 29, 39, 51, 65, ⋯
(differences: +2, +4, +6, +8, +10, +12, +14)

(e) 8, 20, 44, 92, 188, 380, 764, ⋯
(differences: +12, +24, +48, +96, +192, +384)

(f) 5, 17, 53, 161, 485, 1,475, 4,373, ⋯
5 × 3 + 2 = 17
17 × 3 + 2 = 53
53 × 3 + 2 = 161
161 × 3 + 2 = 485
485 × 3 + 2 = 1,457

(g) 2, 25, 140, 715, 3,590, 17,965, ⋯
2 × 5 + 15 = 25
25 × 5 + 15 = 140
140 × 5 + 15 = 715
715 × 5 + 15 = 3,590

(h) 3, 18, 78, 318, 1,278, 5,118, ⋯
3 × 4 + 6 = 18
18 × 4 + 6 = 78
78 × 4 + 6 = 318
318 × 4 + 6 = 1,278

978-1-62399-075-6
Singapore Math Challenge

Page 42

9. (8, 24, 27)
$8 \times 3 = 24$ $24 + 3 = 27$

10. (12, 48, 52)
$12 \times 4 = 48$ $48 + 4 = 52$

Page 43

11.
$50 \times 50 = 2{,}500$
$2{,}500 \times 51 = 127{,}500$
(50, 2,500, 127,500)
$127{,}500 + 2{,}500 + 50 = 130{,}050$

12. $1 + 3 + 5 + 7 + 9 = 25 = 5 \times 5$
$1 + 3 + 5 + 7 + 9 + 11 = 36 = 6 \times 6$

Page 44

13. 3, 8, 15, 24, 35, 48, 63, 80, 99
+5 +7 +9 +11 +13 +15 +17 +19
99, 120, 143, 168, ...
+21 +23 +25

14. $1 + 2 + 3 + 4 + ... + 62 = 63 \times 31$
$= 1{,}953$
1,953 is the last number in the 62nd row.
The first number in the 63rd row is 1,954.
$2{,}007 - 1{,}954 + 1 = 53 + 1$
= 54th number in the 63rd row.
2,007 is in the 63rd row.

Page 45

15. Let the second number be a.
3, (a), (a + 3), (2a + 3), (3a + 6), (5a + 9)
$5a + 9 = 54$
$5a = 54 - 9 = 45$
$a = 45 \div 5 = 9$
The second number is 9.

16. $1 + 2 + 3 + 4 + ... + 29 = 30 \times 14 + 15$
= 435 fractions up to the end when 29 is the denominator.
$435 + 15 = 450$
$\frac{15}{30}$ will be the 450th term.

Chapter 4 Practice

Page 48

1. $12 + 11 \times \square = 12 \times 12$
$11 \times \square = 144 - 12$
$\square = 132 \div 11$
$\square = 12$

2. $\left(\frac{1 + \square}{7} + 4\right) \div 8 = \frac{4}{7}$

$\frac{1 + \square}{7} + 4 = \frac{4}{7} \times 8$

$\frac{1 + \square}{7} = \frac{32}{7} - 4$

$\frac{1 + \square}{7} = \frac{32}{7} - \frac{28}{7} = \frac{4}{7}$

$1 + \square = 4$
$\square = 4 - 1$
$\square = 3$

Page 49

3. $((\square + 4) \times 8) = 40 \times 12$
$\square + 4 = 480 \div 8$
$\square = 60 - 4$
$\square = 56$

4. $\left(\frac{1 + \square}{9} + 3\right) \div 4 = \frac{8}{9}$

$\left(\frac{1 + \square}{9} + 3\right) = \frac{8}{9} \times 4$

$\frac{1 + \square}{9} = \frac{32}{9} - 3$

$\frac{1 + \square}{9} = \frac{32}{9} - \frac{27}{9} = \frac{5}{9}$

$1 + \square = 5$
$\square = 5 - 1$
$\square = 4$

978-1-62399-075-6
Singapore Math Challenge

Page 50

5. $\{((\square - 6) \times 6) + 6\} \div 6 = 6$
$((\square - 6) \times 6) + 6 = 6 \times 6$
$(\square - 6) \times 6 = 36 - 6$
$\square - 6 = 30 \div 6$
$\square = 5 + 6$
$\square = 11$
The value of this number is 11.

6. $\{((\square + 6) \times 3) \div 8\} - 8 = 1$
$((\square + 6) \times 3) \div 8 = 1 + 8$
$(\square + 6) \times 3 = 9 \times 8$
$\square + 6 = 72 \div 3$
$\square = 24 - 6$
$\square = 18$
The number is 18.

Page 51

7. (?) —+ 42→ [ ] —÷ 3→ [ ] —− 36→ [ ] —× 25→ 100
(78) ←− 42— [120] ←× 3— [40] ←+ 36— [4] ←÷ 25— 100
His grandfather's age is 78 years old.

8. (?) —÷ 2→ [ ] —− 4→ [ ] —÷ 2→ [ ] —+ 3→ [ ] —+ 30→ 50
(76) ←× 2— [38] ←+ 4— [34] ←× 2— [17] ←− 3— [20] ←− 30— 50
ABC Megamart had 76 sacks of rice at first.

Page 52

9.

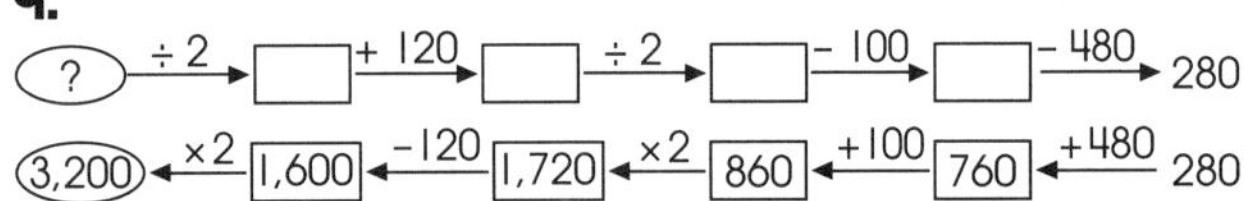

The army of ants had 3,200 g of food at first.

10. (?) —÷ 2→ [ ] —− 20→ [ ] —÷ 2→ [ ] —− 15→ 75
(400) ←× 2— [200] ←+ 20— [180] ←× 2— [90] ←+ 15— 75
ABC Telco carried 400 cell phones at first.

Page 53

11. (?) ←− 6— [ ] ←+ 60— 222
(168) —+ 6→ [162] —− 60→ 222
The actual difference would be 168 if he had read the numbers correctly.

12. Working backward,

$3 - 1 = 2$	$2 \times 2 = 4$
$4 - 1 = 3$	$3 \times 2 = 6$
$6 - 1 = 5$	$5 \times 2 = 10$
$10 - 1 = 9$	$9 \times 2 = 18$
$18 - 1 = 17$	$17 \times 2 = 34$

There were 34 marbles in the bag at first.

Page 54

13.

Alison	32	16	8	52
Beatrice	32	16	56	28
Chloe	32	64	32	16

Alison had 52 books, Beatrice had 28 books and Chloe had 16 books at first.

Page 55

14. $4 \times 2 = 8$ $\qquad 16 \times \frac{5}{4} = 20$

$8 \times \frac{3}{2} = 12$ $\qquad 20 \times \frac{6}{5} = 24$

$12 \times \frac{4}{3} = 16$ $\qquad 24 \times \frac{7}{6} = 28$

28 commuters boarded the bus at the bus station.

Page 56

15.

6th	7th	8th	9th	10th
				100
			100	50
		100	50	25
	100	50	25	2
100	50	25	2	0

$100 + 50 + 25 + 2 = 177$

There were 177 bubbles altogether at the 10th minute.

Page 57

16. Assume there is one bead in each group at the end.

3rd division: (1) + (1) + (1) + (1) + 1

2nd division: (5) + (5) + (5) + (5) + 1

1st division: (21) + (21) + (21) + (21) + 1

$21 + 21 + 21 + 21 + 1 = 85$

The minimum number of beads I have is 85.

Chapter 5 Practice

Page 64

1. $(1 + 100) \times 100 \div 2 = 5{,}050$

2. $(1 + 99) \times 50 \div 2 = 2{,}500$

Page 65

3. $(1 + 50) \times 50 \div 2 = 1{,}275$

4. $5{,}050 + (5{,}050 - 100) = 5{,}050 + 4{,}950$
$= 10{,}000$

Page 66

5. $(1 + 1{,}999) \times 1{,}999 \div 2 = 2{,}000 \times 1{,}999 \div 2$
$= 1{,}000 \times 1{,}999$
$= 1{,}999{,}000$

6. $(298 - 4) \div 3 + 1 = 294 \div 3 + 1$
$= 99$

Number 298 is the 99th term.

Page 67

7. $d = 783 - 775$
$= 15 - 7$
$= 8$

Number of terms $= (783 - 7) \div 8 + 1$
$= 97 + 1$
$= 98$

Sum of the sequence $= (7 + 783) \times 98 \div 2$
$= 38{,}710$

The sum of the sequence is 38,710.

8. 1987 1990 1993 1996 1999 2002 2005
(4th under 1996)

The rest of the books in that series were published in 1987, 1990, 1993, 1999, 2002 and 2005.

Page 68

9. The first number: 4
The last number: 40
Difference, $d = (40 - 4) \div (10 - 1)$
$= 36 \div 9$
$= 4$
The 8 numbers between 4 and 40 are 8, 12, 16, 20, 24, 28, 32 and 36.

10.

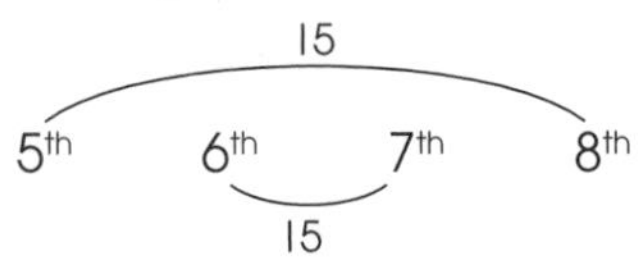

$12 \div 2 = 6$ pairs of 15
$6 \times 15 = 90$
The sum of the number sequence is 90.

Page 69

11. The first number: 12
The fifth number: 60
$d = (60 - 12) \div (5 - 1)$
$= 48 \div 4$
$= 12$
The 3 numbers are 24, 36 and 48.

12. $1 + 2 + 3 + ... + 19 = (1 + 19) \times 19 \div 2$
$= 20 \times 19 \div 2$
$= 10 \times 19$
$= 190$
190 matches were played altogether.

Page 70

13. $d = 2$
Number of terms = 30
30th term = 1st term + $(30 - 1) \times 2$
132 = 1st term + 58
1st term = 132 − 58
1st term = 74
The first row has 74 seats.
$(132 + 74) \times 30 \div 2 = 6,180 \div 2 = 3,090$
There are 3,090 seats altogether in the North Wing of the stadium.

14. Multiples of 11 = 11, 22, 33, 44, 55, 66, 77, 88, 99
$11 + 33 + 55 + 77 + 99 = 110 \times 2 + 55$
110
110
$= 275$
$(1 + 99) \times 50 \div 2 = 2,500$
$2,500 - 275 = 2,225$
The sum of all odd numbers between 1 and 100 that are not divisible by 11 is 2,225.

978-1-62399-075-6
Singapore Math Challenge

Chapter 6 Practice

Page 75

1. (31) 32 33 34 35 36 (37) 38 39 40
(41) 42 (43) 44 45 46 (47) 48 49 50
51 52 (53) 54 55 56 57 58 (59) 60

Page 76

2. 2 + 37 = 39   2 × 37 = 74

The product of the two prime numbers is 74.

3.

1	12	123
(2)	(13)	132
(3)	21	213
	(23)	231
	(31)	312
	32	321

The prime numbers in this list are 2, 3, 13, 23 and 31.

Page 77

4. 5 × 13 = 65   13 + 5 = 18
13 − 5 = 8
The sum of the two prime numbers is 18.
The difference of the two prime numbers is 8.

5. The three prime numbers are likely to be from the numbers below.
2, 3, 5, 7, 11, 13, 17, 19, 23
30 = 2 + 5 + 23 or 30 = 2 + 11 + 17
2 × 5 × 23 = 230 or 2 × 11 × 17 = 374
The group of prime numbers that gives the smallest product is 2, 5 and 23.

Page 78

6.

Numbers before the multiple	Multiples of 6	Numbers after the multiple
65	66	(67)
(71)	72	(73)
77	78	(79)
(83)	84	85
(89)	90	91
95	96	(97)

Observations: Except for 65, 77, 85, 91 and 95, which are multiples of 5 or 7, the rest of the numbers right before and after the multiples of 6 are prime numbers.

Page 79

7. A = 5
5 + 6 = 11, 5 + 8 = 13, 5 + 12 = 17,
5 + 14 = 19

Page 80

8. 50 = 3 + 47   3 × 47 = 141
50 = 7 + 43   7 × 43 = 301
50 = 13 + 37   13 × 37 = 481
50 = 19 + 31   19 × 31 = 589
The biggest possible product of the two prime numbers is 589.

Page 81

9. 27 = 3 + 5 + 19   3 × 5 × 19 = 285
27 = 3 + 7 + 17   3 × 7 × 17 = 357
27 = 3 + 11 + 13   3 × 11 × 13 = 429
The biggest possible product of the 3 prime numbers is 429.

Page 82

10. (a) 91 is not a prime number as it is divisible by 7.
(b) 101 is a prime number.
(c) 119 is not a prime number as it is divisible by 7.
(d) 123 is not a prime number as it is divisible by 3.
(e) 127 is a prime number.
(f) 133 is not a prime number as it is divisible by 7.

978-1-62399-075-6
Singapore Math Challenge

Page 83

11. (a)

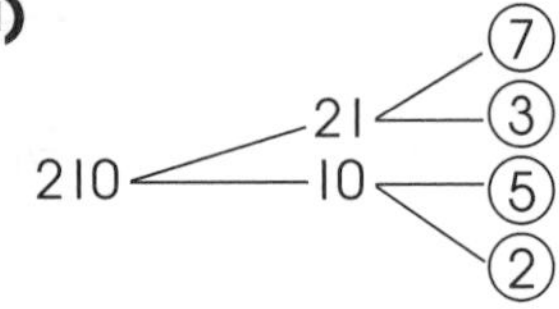

210 = 2 × 3 × 5 × 7

(b)

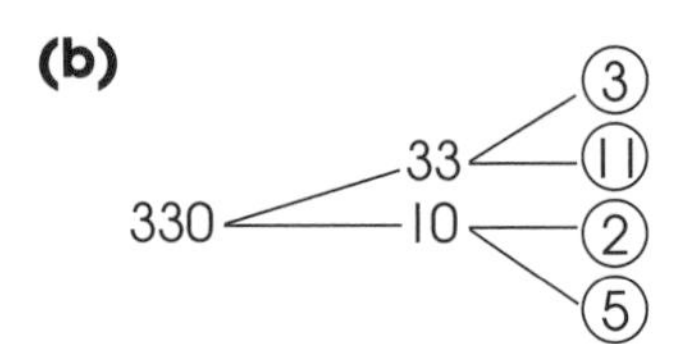

330 = 2 × 3 × 5 × 11

(c)

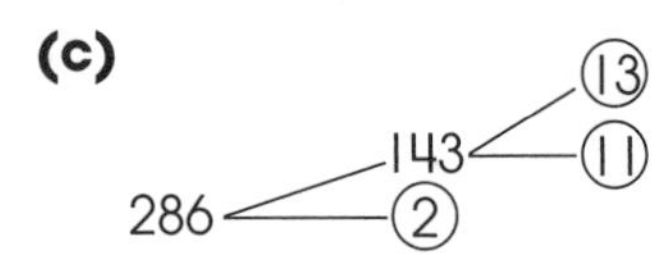

286 = 2 × 11 × 13

(d)

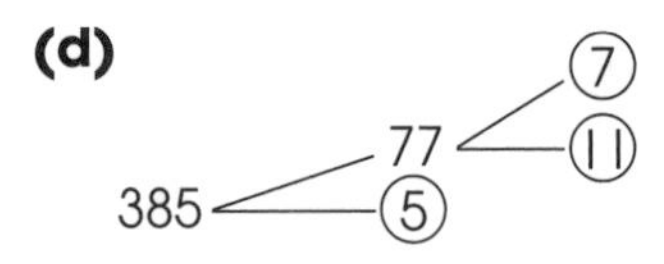

385 = 5 × 7 × 11

(e)

221 — 13, 17

221 = 13 × 17

(f)

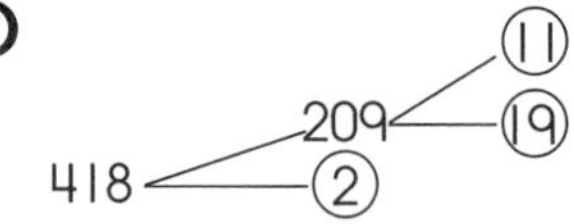

418 = 2 × 11 × 19

(g)

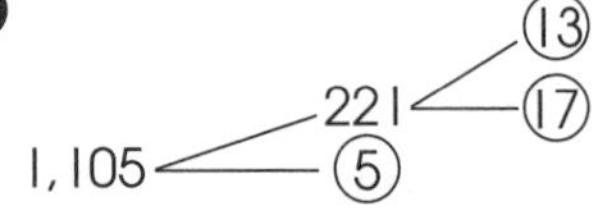

1,105 = 5 × 13 × 17

(h)

1,309 — 187 (11, 17), 7

1,309 = 7 × 11 × 17

Page 85

12. (a) 12 × 12 = 144 (> 137)
Prime numbers smaller than 12 = 2, 3, 5, 7, 11
Since 137 is not divisible by all these prime numbers, 137 is a prime number.

(b) 17 × 17 = 289 (> 271)
Prime numbers smaller than 17 = 2, 3, 5, 7, 11, 13
Since 271 is not divisible by all these prime numbers, 271 is a prime number.

(c) 19 × 19 = 361 (> 337)
Prime numbers smaller than 19 = 2, 3, 5, 7, 11, 13, 17
Since 337 is not divisible by all these prime numbers, 337 is a prime number.

(d) 21 × 21 = 441 (> 437)
Prime numbers smaller than 21 = 2, 3, 5, 7, 11, 13, 17, 19
437 ÷ 19 = 23
437 is not a prime number.

(e) 23 × 23 = 529 (> 507)
We divide 507 by all the prime numbers smaller than 23.
507 ÷ 3 = 169
507 is not a prime number.

(f) 28 × 28 = 784 (> 741)
We divide 741 by all the prime numbers smaller than 28.
741 ÷ 3 = 247
741 is not a prime number.

978-1-62399-075-6
Singapore Math Challenge

Page 86

13.

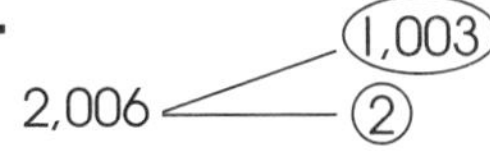

$32 \times 32 = 1{,}024$ (> 1,003)

We divide 1,003 by all the prime numbers smaller than 32.

$1{,}003 \div 17 = 59$

$2{,}006 = 2 \times 17 \times 59$

$2 + 17 + 59 = 78$

The sum of all its prime factors is 78.

14.

1,992 — 996 (2) — 332 (3) — 166 (2) — 83 (2)

$1{,}992 = 2 \times 2 \times 2 \times 3 \times 83$

$2 + 2 + 2 + 3 + 83 = 92$

The sum of all its prime factors is 92.

Page 87

15. ***Method 1: Making a Table***

a	b	c	Area = a × b + b × c
3	5	7	3 × 5 + 5 × 7 = 15 + 35 = 50
5	7	11	5 × 7 + 7 × 11 = 35 + 77 = 112
7	11	13	7 × 11 + 11 × 13 = 77 + 143 = 220

Method 2: Using Equations

$a \times b + b \times c = 220$

$b \times (a + c) = 220$

$b \times (a + c) = 11 \times 20$

$b = 11$

$a + c = 7 + 13 = 20$

$7 \times 13 \times 11 = 1{,}001$

The volume of the rectangular prism is 1,001 cm^3.

Page 88

16.

1,540 — 770 (2) — 77, 10; 77 — (7), (11); 10 — (5), (2)

$1{,}540 = 2 \times 2 \times 5 \times 7 \times 11$

$1{,}540 \times m$ = square number

$1{,}540 \times m = 2 \times 2 \times \_ \times 5 \times \_ \times 7 \times \_ \times 11$

$m = 5 \times 7 \times 11 = 385$

The smallest possible value of m is 385.

Page 89

17.

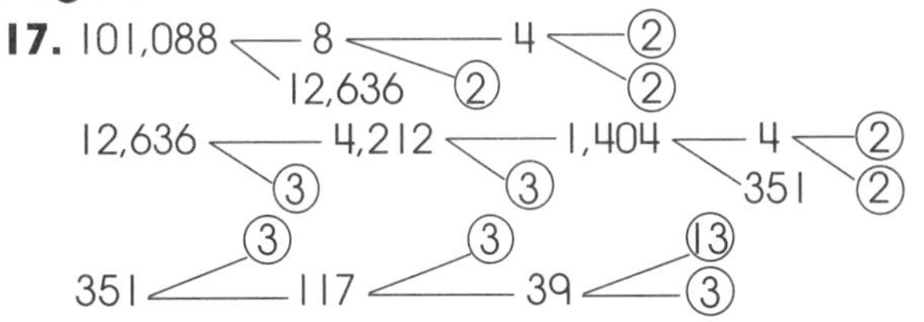

$101{,}088 = 2 \times 2 \times 2 \times 2 \times 2 \times 3 \times 3 \times 3 \times 3 \times 3 \times 13$

Two groups, $2 \times 3 \times 3 \times 13 = 234$

$2 \times 2 \times 2 \times 2 \times 3 \times 3 \times 3 = 432$

$234 + 432 = 666$

The sum of the palindrome pair is 666.

978-1-62399-075-6
Singapore Math Challenge

Page 90

18.

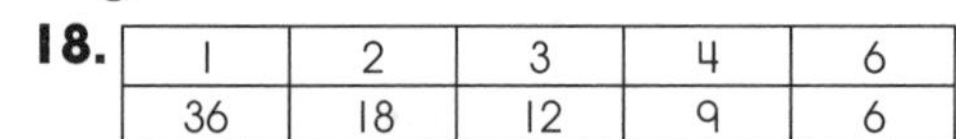

1	2	3	4	6
36	18	12	9	6

5 rectangles of different sizes can be formed from 36 identical rectangles.

19.

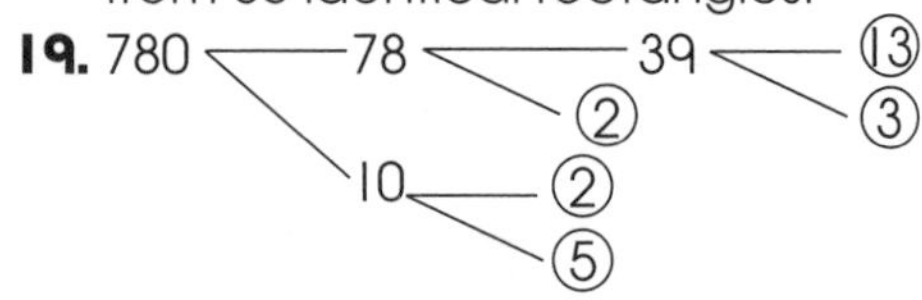

780 = 2 × 2 × 3 × 5 × 13

1,716 — 858 — 429 — 143 — 13; (2) (2) (3) (11)

1,716 = 2 × 2 × 3 × 11 × 13

2 × 2 × 3 × 5 × 13 × a = 2 × 2 × 3 × 11 × 13 × b

The smallest values of a and b are 11 and 5 respectively.

Page 91

20. a + 18 = b + 14 = c + 35

Using guess and check,

a = 19, 19 + 18 = 37, b = 23, 23 + 14 = 37

c = 2, 2 + 35 = 37

19 + 23 + 2 = 44

The value of a + b + c is 44.

Page 92

21. 37 = 3 + 5 + 29   37 = 2 + 5 + 7 + 23

37 = 3 + 11 + 23   37 = 2 + 3 + 13 + 19

37 = 5 + 13 + 19   37 = 2 + 5 + 11 + 19

37 = 7 + 11 + 19   37 = 2 + 5 + 13 + 17

37 = 7 + 13 + 17   37 = 2 + 7 + 11 + 17

37 is a sum of 3 or more prime numbers in 10 ways.

Chapter 7 Practice

Page 101

1. **(a)** 2 + 3 + 6 + 7 = 18

2,367 is divisible by 3 and by 9.

(b) 1 + 0 + 0 + 0 + 2 = 3

10,002 is divisible by 3 but not by 9.

(c) 1 + 8 + 1 + 3 + 5 = 18

18,135 is divisible by 3 and by 9.

(d) 1 + 0 + 0 + 3 + 2 = 6

10,032 is divisible by 3 but not by 9.

Page 102

2. 5 + 1 + 5 + 4 = 15

4 + 5 + 1 + 5 = 15

5,154 is divisible by 3.

Its palindromic number, 4515, is also divisible by 3 as the sum of all the digits is the same and can be divided by 3.

3. Yes, but the last digit must be 5.

Page 103

4. No, it is not possible.

Page 104

5. **(a)** 41 − 15 = 26

15,041 is divisible by 13 but not by 7.

(b) 523 − 397 = 126

126 ÷ 7 = 18

397,523 is divisible by 7 but not by 13.

(c) 597 − 415 = 182

182 ÷ 13 = 14

182 ÷ 7 = 26

415,597 is divisible by 7 and by 13.

(d) 508 − 417 = 91

91 ÷ 13 = 7

91 ÷ 7 = 13

417,508 is divisible by 7 and by 13.

978-1-62399-075-6

Page 105

6. 4 + 5 + 6 + 7 + 6 + 5 + 4 = 37
It is not divisible by 9.
(4 + 6 + 6 + 4) − (5 + 7 + 5)
= 20 − 17
= 3
It is not divisible by 11 either.

Page 106

7. **(a)** (8 + 6 + 3) − (3 + 6 + 8)
= 17 − 17
= 0
386,683 is divisible by 11.

(b) (5 + 6 + 1) − (1 + 6 + 5)
= 12 − 12
= 0
156,651 is divisible by 11.

(c) (3 + 8 + 7 + 2) − (2 + 7 + 8 + 3)
= 20 − 20
= 0
23,788,732 is divisible by 11.

(d) (2 + 4 + 3 + 1) − (1 + 3 + 4 + 2)
= 10 − 10
= 0
12,344,321 is divisible by 11.

To conclude, a palindrome with an even number of digits is divisible by 11 as the difference of their sums will be 0.

Page 107

8. 3,466 − 645 = 2,821
821 − 2 = 819
819 ÷ 13 = 63
3,466,645 is divisible by 13.

Page 108

9. 123 (3-digit number)
123,123 (6-digit number)
123,123 ÷ 13 = 9,471
9,471 ÷ 11 = 861
861 ÷ 7 = 123
I will get back the original 3-digit number.
Reason: 7 × 11 × 13 = 1,001
1,001 × any 3-digit number
= 6-digit number with the 3-digit number repeated.

Page 109

10. **(a)** 1 + 2 + 7 + 8 = 18
1,278 is divisible by 3 and by 9.

(b) 4 + 6 + 3 + 2 = 15
4,632 is divisible by 3 but not by 9.

(c) 5 + 4 + 6 + 8 + 4 = 27
54,684 is divisible by 3 and by 9.

(d) 1 + 1 + 9 + 3 + 7 + 5 = 26
119,375 is not divisible by 3 or by 9.

Page 110

11. **(a)** 37,625 is divisible by 25 and by 125.
It is not divisible by 4 or by 8.

(b) 93,648 is divisible by 4 and by 8.
It is not divisible by 25 or by 125.

(c) 87,615 is not divisible by 4, by 8, by 25 or by 125.

(d) 1,548,672 is divisible by 4 and by 8.
It is not divisible by 25 or by 125.

Page 111

12. 517,699
699 − 517 = 182
182 ÷ 13 = 14
182 ÷ 7 = 26
517,699 is divisible by 7 and by 13.

978-1-62399-075-6
Singapore Math Challenge

Page 112

13. $5 + 0 + 1 + 5 = 11$
$m = 12 - 11 = 1$
$m = 15 - 11 = 4$
$m = 18 - 11 = 7$
The possible values of m are 1, 4 and 7.

Page 113

14. Since $15 = 3 \times 5$, b can only be 0 or 5.
When b = 0,
$a + 7 + 8 + 8 + 9 + 0 = a + 32$
For a + 32 to be divided by 3,
$a = 1, 4, 7$
Therefore, the possible values of the number are 178,890, 478,890 and 778,890.
When b = 5,
$a + 7 + 8 + 8 + 9 + 5 = a + 37$
For a + 37 to be divided by 3,
$a = 2, 5, 8$
Therefore, the possible values of the number can also be 278,895, 578,895 and 878,895.

15. 333,333
$333 - 333 = 0$
Since 0 is divisible by 7, 333,333 is divisible by 7.
888,888
$888 - 888 = 0$
888,888 is divisible by 7.
The possible values of a must either be 0 or 7.

Page 114

16. The last 2 digits of 2,006,☐☐☐ have to be 00 so as to be divisible by 4 and by 25.
We have 2,006,☐00.
$2 + 0 + 0 + 6 + \square + 0 + 0 = 8$
$\square = 1, 4, 7$
The possible values of this number are 2,006,100, 2,006,400 and 2,006,700.

17. Since it is the largest possible number, the first digit must be 9.
$(9 + 9 + 9) - (8 + 4 + \square) = 11$
$27 - (12 + \square) = 11$
$\square = 4$
The largest possible number is 989,494.

Page 115

18. The ones digit of the number must be 0 or 5 in order to be divisible by 5.
When it is 0, we have 25,☐40.
$2 + 5 + 4 + 0 = 11$ $\square = 1, 4, 7$
Therefore, the possible values are 25,140, 25,440 and 25,740.
When it is 5, we have 25,☐45.
$2 + 5 + 4 + 5 = 16$ $\square = 2, 5, 8$
Therefore, the possible values are 25,245, 25,545 and 25,845.

19. $(100 - 1) \div 3 = 99 \div 3 = 33$ multiples of 3
$(100 - 1) \div 11 = 99 \div 11 = 9$ multiples of 11
33, 66 and 99 are multiples of both 3 and 11.
$100 - 33 - 9 + 3 = 61$
61 whole numbers between 1 and 100 are not divisible by 3 or by 11.

Page 116

20. $112 - 35 = 77$
35,112 is divisible by 7 and by 11 but not by 13.

21. The ones digit can only be 0 or 5.
When it is 0, we have 5☐,340.
$5 + 3 + 4 + 0 = 12$
☐ = 18 − 12 = 6
When it is 5, we have 5☐,345.
$5 + 3 + 4 + 5 = 17$
☐ = 18 − 17 = 1
The possible values of ☐ are 6 and 1.
The possible values of the number are 56,340 and 51,345.

Page 117

22. The last two digits must be 00 in order to be divisible by 4 and by 25.
We have 368,☐00.
$3 + 6 + 8 + 0 + 0 = 17$
☐ = 18 − 17 = 1
The smallest possible number is 368,100.

23. We have 8☐☐,☐☐☐.
We choose the smallest digits, 0, 1, 2 and 3, to fill in.
801,23☐
$8 + 1 + 2 + 3 = 14$
☐ = 18 − 14 = 4
The smallest possible value of this number is 801,234.

Chapter 8 Practice

Page 122

1. From the last clue, we can rule out 1, 4, 5, 6.
~~4~~ ~~6~~ 0 7
~~1~~ 3 8 ~~5~~
~~2~~ 8 7 ~~9~~
(2 numbers are in the correct position.)
The answers could be 3,870 or 0,873.
Since 0,873 is a 3-digit number, the number was 3,870.

Page 123

2. If Box A has the wrong label, it contains blue marbles. This indicates that Box B has the wrong label too, because only one box has blue marbles. It also means that Box C has the wrong label. We will then have a scenario of three wrong labels, so Box A cannot be the one having the wrong label.
If Box A has the right label, Box B and Box C will have the wrong labels.
Box A → white marbles
Box B → white marbles
Box C → blue marbles
Box C contains blue marbles.

Page 124

3. $48 = 2 \times 4 \times 6$ $16 = 3 + 5 + 8$
$63 = 1 \times 7 \times 9$
The largest number among Jolene's cards is 8.

Page 125

4. Last number in the 14th row
$= 1 + 2 + 3 + 4 + \ldots + 13 + 14 = 105$
106, 107, 108, 109, (110), 111, ...
The 5th number in the 15th row is 110.

Page 126

5. When Ashley is 10 years old, Stella is 13 years old and Melanie is 9 years old.
This fits the statement where each girl makes one incorrect statement.

Page 127

6. ***Method 1: Solve by Drawing***
○ is dry weather ● is wet weather
"There were 14 dry mornings."
Morning ○○○○○○○○○○○○○○
"There were 8 dry afternoons."
Morning ○○○○○○○○○○○○○○
Afternoon ○○○○○○○○
"It rained 10 times ..."
●●○○○○○○○○○○○○○○
○○○○○○○○●●●●●●●●
Method 2: Solve by Reasoning
$(10 + 8 + 14) \div 2 = 16$
The meteorologist recorded 16 days.

Page 128

7.

	Andy	Kevin	Matthew
Police officer			×
Doctor	×	×	✓
Teacher			

Matthew, the doctor, is older than the police officer.
Since the doctor is younger than Kevin, Kevin is not the police officer.
Kevin is the teacher.

Page 129

8. If Leon told the truth, then Peter also told the truth. So, Teddy lied. Leon and Peter both told the truth.

Page 130

9.

	Amanda	Beatrice	Jodie
Town A			
Town B			×
Town C	×	×	✓

Jodie is older than the lady from Town B.
Jodie is younger than Beatrice.
Beatrice is not from Town B.
Beatrice comes from Town A.

Page 131

10. $23 \times 4 + 19 \times 2 = 130$
Dave scores 4 sets of 23 and 2 sets of 19.

Page 132

11. If Colin did it, he would be lying. Jason and David would also be lying. Only Melvin told the truth.
So, Colin was the culprit.

Page 133

12. Herman's wife cannot be Alicia, Beatrice or Elaine.
Charles's wife cannot be Beatrice or Elaine.
David's wife cannot be Elaine.
The four couples are Herman and Florence, Charles and Alicia, David and Beatrice, and Graham and Elaine.

Page 134

13. A → Chinese → 16th
D → Egyptian → 10th
C → German → 8th
B → Mexican → 4th

978-1-62399-075-6
Singapore Math Challenge

Page 135

14.

	Greenville	Bloomsberry	Windschill
Melissa	×	✓	
Amy	×	×	✓
Tony	✓		

	Swimming	Basketball	Volleyball
Melissa	×		✓
Amy	×	✓	
Tony	✓	×	×

Melissa comes from Bloomsberry and likes volleyball. Amy comes from Windschill and likes basketball. Tony comes from Greenville and likes swimming.

OR

	Greenville	Bloomsberry	Windschill
Melissa	×	×	✓
Amy	✓	×	×
Tony	×	✓	×

	Swimming	Basketball	Volleyball
Melissa	×	✓	×
Amy	✓	×	×
Tony	×	×	✓

Melissa comes from Windschill and likes basketball. Amy comes from Greenville and likes swimming. Tony comes from Bloomsberry and likes volleyball.

Chapter 9 Practice

Page 142

1. Let the first number be a.

$a + (a + 1) + (a + 2) + (a + 3) + (a + 4) = 465$

$5a = 465 - 10 = 455$

$a = 455 \div 5 = 91$

The five consecutive numbers are 91, 92, 93, 94 and 95.

Page 143

2. Let the number of students be p.

$4p + 48 = 6p - 8$

$48 + 8 = 6p - 4p$

$2p = 56$

$p = 56 \div 2 = 28$

She gives the candy to 28 students.

Page 144

3.

US \$1.00 → Singapore \$1.45

Singapore \$50 → 1,000 Thai Baht

Singapore \$1.00 → 20 Thai Baht

Singapore \$1.45 → 29 Thai Baht

29,000 Thai Baht → US \$1,000

29,000 Thai Baht could buy 1,000 US dollars on that day.

Page 145

4. Let f and v be football and volleyball respectively.

$4f + 4v \rightarrow \$240$

$3f + 5v \rightarrow \$234$

$12f + 12v \rightarrow 3 \times \$240 = \$720$

$12f + 20v \rightarrow 4 \times \$234 = \$936$

$8v \rightarrow \$936 - \$720 = \$216$

$v \rightarrow \$216 \div 8 = \$27$

$3f \rightarrow \$234 - 5 \times \$27 = \$99$

$f \rightarrow \$99 \div 3 = \$33$

The cost of a football is \$33.
The cost of a volleyball is \$27.

978-1-62399-075-6
Singapore Math Challenge

Page 146

5. Let the numbers of long tubes and short tubes be m and n respectively.

$$5 \times m + 3 \times n = 62$$
$$5m + 3n = 62$$
$$5m = 62 - 3n$$
$$m = \frac{62 - 3n}{5}$$

One possible answer:
When $n = 4$,

$$m = \frac{62 - 3 \times 4}{5} = 10$$

Another possible answer:
When $n = 9$,

$$m = \frac{62 - 3 \times 9}{5} = 7$$

Page 147

6. Let the number of chickens and rabbits be c and r respectively.

$c + r = 145$ .... (1)

A chicken has 2 legs and a rabbit has 4 legs.

$2c + 4r = 410$ .... (2)

(1) × 2

$2c + 2r = 145 \times 2 = 290$ .... (3)

(2) − (3)

$$2c + 4r - 2c - 2r = 410 - 290$$
$$2r = 120$$
$$r = 120 \div 2 = 60$$

Substituting $r = 60$ into (1),

$$c + 60 = 145$$
$$c = 145 - 60 = 85$$

The farmer has 85 chickens and 60 rabbits.

Page 148

7. Let the numbers of big boxes and small boxes be b and s respectively.

$$12 \times b + 5 \times s = 99$$
$$12b + 5s = 99$$
$$12b = 99 - 5s$$
$$b = \frac{99 - 5s}{12}$$

One possible answer:
When $s = 3$,

$$b = \frac{99 - 5 \times 3}{12} = 7$$

Another possible answer:
When $s = 15$,

$$b = \frac{99 - 5 \times 15}{12} = 2$$

Page 149

8. Let the month of his birthday be m and the day of his birthday be d.

$$31 \times m + 12 \times d = 213$$
$$12d = 213 - 31m$$
$$d = \frac{213 - 31m}{12}$$

When $m = 3$,

$$d = \frac{213 - 31 \times 3}{12} = \frac{120}{12} = 10$$

Jonathan's birthday is on March 10th.

Page 150

9. $A + B + C = 31$ .... (1)

$C + D + E = 47$ .... (2)

$A + B + D + E = 64$ .... (3)

(1) + (2)

$A + B + 2C + D + E = 78$ .... (4)

(4) − (3)

$$2C = 14$$
$$C = 7$$

Page 151

10. Let f, b and d be fries, burger and drink respectively.

$3f + 2b + 1d \rightarrow \$10.95$
$1f + 2b + 3d \rightarrow \$11.25$
$4f + 4b + 4d \rightarrow \$10.95 + \$11.25 = \$22.20$
$f + b + d \rightarrow \$22.20 \div 4 = \$5.55$

The price of a set of items is \$5.55.

Page 152

11. ⊡ + ⁘ + ⊙ + ⊙ = 52 .... (1)
⊡ + ⁘ + ⁘ + ⊙ = 47 .... (2)
⊡ + ⊡ + ⁘ + ⊙ = 49 .... (3)

Compare (1) and (2)
⊙ = ⁘ + 5

Compare (2) and (3)
⊡ = ⁘ + 2

Replace ⊙ and ⊡ in (2) by (⁘ + 5) and (⁘ + 2) respectively.

⁘ + 2 + ⁘ + ⁘ + ⁘ + 5 = 47
4 ⁘ = 40
⁘ = 10
⊙ = 15
⊡ = 12

Page 153

12. $3A + 7B + 1C \rightarrow \$31.50$
$4A + 10B + 1C \rightarrow \$42$

By comparison,
$1A + 3B \rightarrow \$42 - \$31.50 = \$10.50$
$2A + 6B \rightarrow \$2 \times \$10.50 = \$21$

Again by comparison,
$1A + 1B + 1C \rightarrow \$31.50 - \$21 = \$10.50$

The price of item A + item B + item C is \$10.50.

Page 154

13. Let a, b and c be the numbers of years the 3 numbers of different questions were used.

We have
$a + b + c = 20$ .... (1)
$20a + 25b + 30c = 515$ .... (2)

(1) × 20
$20a + 20b + 20c = 400$ .... (3)

(2) − (3)
$5b + 10c = 115$
$5b = 115 - 10c$
$$b = \frac{115 - 10c}{5}$$

One possible answer:
When $c = 8$,
$$b = \frac{115 - 10 \times 8}{5} = 7$$

Another possible answer:
When $c = 10$,
$$b = \frac{115 - 10 \times 10}{5} = 3$$

Page 155

14. Let a, b and c be the number of roosters, hens and chicks respectively.

$a + b + c = 100$ .... (1)

$5a + 3b + \frac{c}{3} = 100$ .... (2)

(2) × 3

$15a + 9b + c = 300$ .... (3)

(3) – (1)

$14a + 8b = 200$

$14a = 200 - 8b$

$a = \frac{200 - 8b}{14}$

One possible answer:
When $b = 4$,

$a = \frac{200 - 8 \times 4}{14}$

$= 12$

$c = 100 - 4 - 12$

$= 84$

Another possible answer:
When $b = 11$,

$a = \frac{200 - 8 \times 11}{14}$

$= 8$

$c = 100 - 11 - 8$

$= 81$

Chapter 10 Practice

Page 162

1. $7 \times 6 + 6 = 48$ $\quad$ $7 \times 5 + 5 = 40$

$7 \times 4 + 4 = 32$ $\quad$ $7 \times 3 + 3 = 24$

$7 \times 2 + 2 = 16$ $\quad$ $7 \times 1 + 1 = 8$

6 numbers have the same quotient and remainder when divided by 7.

Page 163

2.

Sun.	Mon.	Tue.	Wed.	Thu.	Fri.	Sat.
				1	2	3
R4	R5	R6	R0	R1	R2	R3

$31 + 28 + 31 + 1 = 91$

$91 \div 7 = 13 \text{ R } 0$

April 1st was a Wednesday in that year.

Page 164

3.

Sun.	Mon.	Tue.	Wed.	Thu.	Fri.	Sat.
					Today	
R3	R4	R5	R6	R0	R1	R2

$90 \div 7 = 12 \text{ R } 6$

It will be a Wednesday 90 days later.

Page 165

4. Multiples of 7 = 7, 14, 21, 28, 35, 42, 49, 56, 63, 70, ...

(Multiples of 7) + 5 = 12, 19, 26, 33, 40, 47, 54, (61), 68, 75, ...

Multiples of 9 = 9, 18, 27, 36, 45, 54, 63, 72, ...

(Multiples of 9) + 7 = 16, 25, 34, 43, 52, (61), 70, ...

The 2-digit number is 61.

Page 166

5. 5 black: R1, R2, R3, R4, R5

4 blue: R6, R7, R8, R9

3 white: R10, R11, R0

$5 + 4 + 3 = 12$

$150 \div 12 = 12 \text{ R } 6$

The color of the 150th bead is blue.

$4 \times 12 + 1 = 49$

There are 49 blue beads in the first 150 beads.

Page 167

6. $3 + 7 + 2 + 1 + 5 + 2 = 20$
$122 \div 6 = 20 \text{ R } 2$
$20 \times 20 + 3 + 7 = 410$
The sum of the first 122 numbers is 410.

3	7	2	1	5	2
R1	R2	R3	R4	R5	R0

$138 \div 6 = 23 \text{ R } 0$
The 138th number is 2.

Page 168

7. $30 + 31 + 30 = 91$

Sun.	Mon.	Tue.	Wed.	Thu.	Fri.	Sat.
					1	2
R3	R4	R5	R6	R0	R1	R2

$91 \div 7 = 13 \text{ R } 0$
August 30th was a Thursday in that year.

Page 169

8. $120 \div 18 = 6 \text{ R } 12$ $\quad$ $144 \div 18 = 8$
The smallest possible value of the 2-digit number is 18.

Page 170

9.

A	B	C	D	E	F	G
R1	R2	R3	R4	R5	R6	R0

$1{,}986 \div 7 = 283 \text{ R } 5$
Region E received the 1,986th rescue package.
$1{,}976 \div 7 = 282 \text{ R } 2$
$282 + 1 = 283$
Region B had received 283 rescue packages by the time the 1,976th package was handed out.

Page 171

10. $A \div B = 7 \text{ R } 20$ $\quad$ $A = 7B + 20$
$A + B = 340$
$7B + 20 + B = 340$
$8B = 340 - 20 = 320$
$B = 320 \div 8 = 40$
$A + 40 = 340$
$A = 340 - 40 = 300$
The two numbers are 300 and 40.

Page 172

11. The least common multiple of 2, 3, 4, 5 and 6 is 60.

Page 173

12. (Multiples of 4) + 2 = 6, 10, 14, 18, 22, 26, 30, 34, 38, 42, 46, (50), 54, 58, 62
(Multiples of 3) + 2 = 5, 8, 11, 14, 17, 20, 23, 26, 29, 32, 35, 38, 41, 44, 47, (50), 53, 56
(Multiples of 7) + 1 = 8, 15, 22, 29, 36, 43, (50), 57, 64, ...
The smallest possible value of this number is 50.

Page 174

13. Divisor + Dividend = $171 - 12 - 8 = 151$
Let A be the divisor and B be the dividend.
$A + B = 151$ $\quad$ $B = A \times 12 + 8$
$A + B = 151$
$A + A \times 12 + 8 = 151$
$13A + 8 = 151$
$13A = 151 - 8 = 143$
$A = 143 \div 13 = 11$
$171 - 12 - 8 - 11 = 140$
The dividend is 140 and the divisor is 11.

978-1-62399-075-6
Singapore Math Challenge

Page 175

14. $5 + 3 + 4 = 12$

$160 \div 12 = 13 \text{ R } 4$

R1 R2 R3 R4 R5 R6 R7 R8 R9 R10 R11 R12

(R1–R5: red; R6–R7: white; R8–R12: black)

The last bead is red.

$13 \times 5 + 4 = 69$

There are 69 red beads.

Page 176

15. Since the string of numbers is a multiple of 6, we look at 333,333 alone.

$333{,}333 \div 7 = 47{,}619$

$\underbrace{333 \ldots 333}_{12 \text{ digits}} \div 7 = 47{,}619{,}047{,}619$

There is no remainder and the last digit of the quotient is 9.

Page 177

16. $111{,}111 \div 7 = 15{,}873$

$\underbrace{111 \ldots 111}_{24 \text{ digits}} \div 7 = \underbrace{15{,}873 \ldots 015{,}873}_{23 \text{ digits}}$

There is no remainder and the last digit of the quotient is 3.

Chapter 11 Practice

Page 183

1. ***Method 1: Solve by Reasoning***

Total mass of 3 people
$= 3 \times 60 = 180$ kg

Total mass of 4 people
$= 4 \times 57 = 228$ kg

$228 - 180 = 48$ kg

Method 2: Solve by Drawing

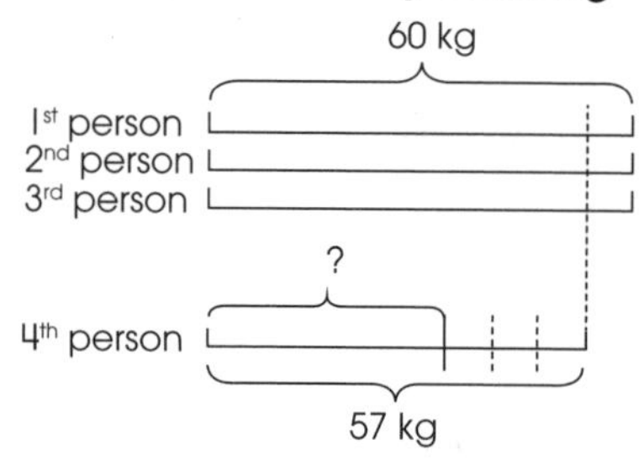

$60 - 57 = 3$

$3 \times 3 = 9$

$57 - 9 = 48$

The mass of the last person was 48 kg.

Page 184

2. $3 \times 120 = 360$

$4 \times 110 = 440$

$440 - 360 = 80$

80 must be added so that the average will become 110.

Page 185

3. Highest = 95

Lowest = 75

$\frac{77 + 82 + 78 + 83}{4} = 80$

The average test score, without considering the highest and the lowest scores, is 80.

Page 186

4. $1,590 - 1,470 = 120$

$120 \div 40 = 3$

Each thumbtack weighed 3 g.

$1,590 \div 3 = 530$

There were 530 thumbtacks in the box at first.

Page 187

5. $5 \times 20 = 100$

$5 \times 18 = 90$

$100 - 90 = 10$

$10 + 4 = 14$

The original value of the changed number is 14.

Page 188

6. $\frac{32 + 40 + 41 + m + 50}{5} = 45$

$166 + m = 45 \times 5 = 225$

$m = 225 - 166 = 59$

The value of m is 59.

Page 189

7. $A = 2 + B$ .... (1)

$B = 11 + C$ .... (2)

From (2), $C = B - 11$ .... (3)

$A + B + C = 3 \times 70$

$2 + B + B + B - 11 = 210$

$3B = 210 + 11 - 2$

$3B = 219$

$B = 219 \div 3 = 73$

$A = 73 + 2 = 75$

$C = 73 - 11 = 62$

The values of A, B and C are 73, 75 and 62 respectively.

Page 190

8. $\frac{83 + 66 + 74 + 73}{4} = 74$

$74 + 12 = 86$

She read 86 pages on the fifth day.

Page 191

9. $\frac{A + B}{2} = 50$ $\qquad$ $\frac{B + C}{2} = 43$

$\frac{A + C}{2} = 45$

$A + B = 100$

$B + C = 86$

$A + C = 90$

$2A + 2B + 2C = 100 + 86 + 90 = 276$

$A + B + C = 276 \div 2 = 138$

$\frac{A + B + C}{3} = 138 \div 3 = 46$

The average of A, B and C is 46.

Page 192

10. Let the average number of pages Joseph read during the five days be m.

$\frac{83 + 65 + 60 + 84}{4} = 73$

$\frac{73 \times 4 + (m + 8)}{5} = m$

$292 + m + 8 = 5m$

$292 + 8 = 5m - m = 4m$

$m = 300 \div 4 = 75$

$75 + 8 = 83$

He read 83 pages of the book on day 5.

978-1-62399-075-6
Singapore Math Challenge

Page 193

11. Let Eugene's mass be m.

Eugene = m
Ken = m + 6
David $= \frac{m + m + 6}{2} + 6 = \frac{2m + 6}{2} + 6$
$= m + 3 + 6$
$= m + 9$

$m + m + 6 + m + 9 = 126$
$3m = 126 - 6 - 9 = 111$
$m = 111 \div 3 = 37$

$37 + 9 = 46$

David's mass is 46 kg.

Page 194

12. $100 - 86 = 14$ points

14 points are needed for Matthew's average score to improve from 84 to 86.

$86 - 84 = 2$
$14 \div 2 = 7$
$7 + 1 = 8$

There are 8 English tests altogether in this year.

Page 195

13. Common multiple of 30 and 60 = 180 km

Time taken to travel from Town A to Town B = $180 \div 30 = 6$ hours

Time taken to return from Town B = $180 \div 60 = 3$ hours

Total time for the two trips = $6 + 3 = 9$ hours

Total distance = $2 \times 180 = 360$ km

$360 \div 9 = 40$ km/h

The average driving speed for the two trips was 40 km/h.

Page 196

14. $\frac{A + B}{2} = 8$ $\frac{B + C}{2} = 3.6$

$\frac{C + D}{2} = 5.8$

$A + B = 16$ .... (1)
$B + C = 7.2$ .... (2)
$C + D = 11.6$ .... (3)

(1) − (2)

$A + B - (B + C) = 16 - 7.2$
$A - C = 8.8$ .... (4)

(4) + (3)

$A - C + C + D = 8.8 + 11.6$
$A + D = 20.4$

$\frac{A + D}{2} = 20.4 \div 2 = 10.2$

The average of A and D is 10.2.

Page 197

15. Total mass of children = $7 \times 36 = 252$ kg

Total mass of girls = $3 \times 32 = 96$ kg

Total mass of boys = $252 - 96 = 156$ kg

$156 \div 4 = 39$ kg

The average mass of the boys is 39 kg.

Chapter 12 Practice

Page 203

1.

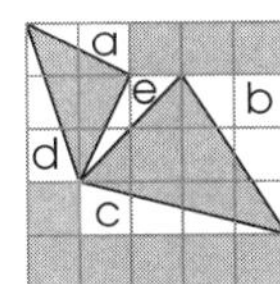

Number of ▢ squares = 9
Area of the 9 ▢ squares
$= 1 \times 1 \times 9 = 9\ cm^2$

Area of Δ a $= \frac{1}{2} \times 2 \times 1 = 1\ cm^2$

Area of Δ b $= \frac{1}{2} \times 2 \times 3 = 3\ cm^2$

Area of Δ c $= \frac{1}{2} \times 4 \times 1 = 2\ cm^2$

Area of Δ d $= \frac{1}{2} \times 1 \times 3 = 1.5\ cm^2$

Area of Δ e = $\times 1 \times 2 = 1\ cm^2$
$5 \times 5 - 9 - 1 - 3 - 2 - 1.5 - 1 = 7.5\ cm^2$
The total area of the shaded regions is $7.5\ cm^2$.

Page 204

2. Area of $\Delta DGC = \frac{1}{4}$ of parallelogram ABCD

$6 \times 3 = 18\ cm^2$
$4 \times 18 = 72\ cm^2$
The area of ABCD is $72\ cm^2$.

Page 205

3.

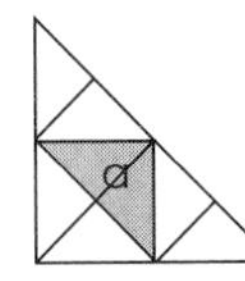

Area of Δ a $= \frac{1}{2} \times 5 \times 2.5$
$= 6.25\ cm^2$
$3 \times 6.25 = 18.75\ cm^2$

The area of the shaded region is $18.75\ cm^2$.

Page 206

4. Look for the difference of two square numbers.
4, 9, 16, 25, 36, 49, 64, 81, 100, 121, 144, 169, ...
$144 - 49 = 95\ cm^2$
The sides of the two squares are 12 cm and 7 cm.
$12 \times 3 + 7 \times 3 + 12 - 7 = 62$ cm
The perimeter of the figure is 62 cm.

Page 207

5. AG + EC = 5 + 5 = 10 cm
$(10 - 8) \times 8 = 16\ cm^2$
The area of the shaded rectangle EFGH is $16\ cm^2$.

Page 208

6.

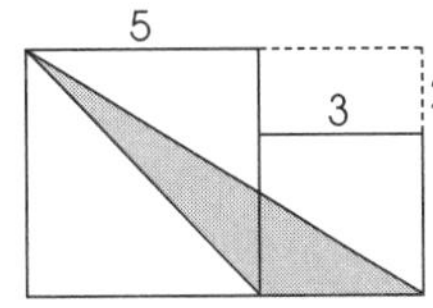

Treat the whole figure as a rectangle.

Area of rectangle
$= 8 \times 5 = 40\ cm^2$

$40 - (\frac{1}{2} \times 5 \times 5) - (\frac{1}{2} \times 8 \times 5) = 7.5\ cm^2$
The area of the shaded region is $7.5\ cm^2$.

Page 209

7. Total area $= 6 \times 6 + 4 \times 4 = 52\ cm^2$

Area of Δ ABC $= \frac{1}{2} \times 6 \times 6 = 18\ cm^2$

Area of Δ CEF $= \frac{1}{2} \times 10 \times 4 = 20\ cm^2$
$52 - 18 - 20 = 14\ cm^2$
The area of the shaded region is $14\ cm^2$.

978-1-62399-075-6
Singapore Math Challenge

Page 210

8. Area of square = $10 \times 10 = 100$ cm^2

Area of two small triangles $= 2 \times \frac{1}{2} \times 3 \times 3$
$= 9$ cm^2

Area of two big triangles $= 2 \times \frac{1}{2} \times 7 \times 7$
$= 49$ cm^2

$100 - 9 - 49 = 42$ cm^2

The area of the rectangle that is embedded in the square is 42 cm^2.

Page 211

9.

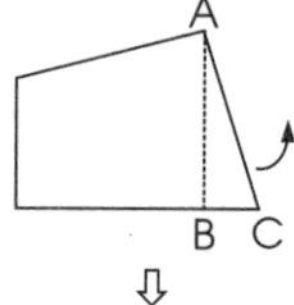

Cut along AB and flip ΔABC 270°.

⇩

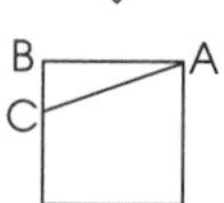

Area of quadrilateral
$= 12 \times 12$
$= 144$ cm^2

Page 212

10. Area of the biggest square $= 12 \times 12 = 144$ cm^2

$144 \div 2 = 72$ cm^2
$72 \div 2 = 36$ cm^2
$36 \div 2 = 18$ cm^2
$18 \div 2 = 9$ cm^2
$9 \div 2 = 4.5$ cm^2

The area of the shaded region is 4.5 cm^2.

Page 213

11. Area of the 2nd square
$= 4 \times 4$
$= 16$ cm^2

Area of the 3rd square
$= 16 \div 2$
$= 8$ cm^2

Total area of the shaded regions
$= 2.5 \times \frac{8}{9} = \frac{20}{9}$

Area of the biggest square
$= 4 \times 8$
$= 32$ cm^2

Total area of the shaded regions : Area of the biggest square
$= \frac{20}{9} : 32$
$= 20 : 288$
$= 5 : 72$

Page 214

12. $\frac{1}{2}$ of square ABCD $= 252 \div 2 = 126$ cm^2

x is half of 126 cm^2 (or ΔABD).

$x = 126 \div 2 = 63$ cm^2

y is $\frac{4}{9}$ of ΔBCD if we can section it into 9 equal parts.

$y = \frac{4}{9} \times 126 = 56$ cm^2

The values of x and y are 63 cm^2 and 56 cm^2 respectively.

Page 215

13. <u>Scenario 1: A and B do not overlap at all.</u>

The difference of areas
$= 6 \times 6 - 5 \times 5 = 11$ cm^2

<u>Scenario 2: Entire B is inside A.</u>

The difference of areas
$= 6 \times 6 - 5 \times 5 = 11$ cm^2

<u>Scenario 3: Half of B overlaps A.</u>

The difference of areas
$= (6 \times 6 - \frac{1}{2} \times 5 \times 5) - (5 \times 5 - \frac{1}{2} \times 5 \times 5)$
$= 11$ cm^2

The difference of the two shaded areas is 11 cm^2.

Page 216

14. $112 - 11 - 17 = 84$

$84 \times \frac{11}{11 + 17} = 33$

$84 \times \frac{17}{11 + 17} = 51$

The area of the biggest plot of land is 51 hectares.

978-1-62399-075-6
Singapore Math Challenge

Page 217

15.

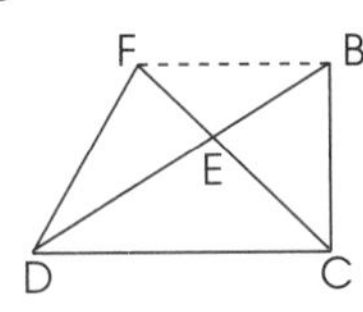

Area of ΔCDF = Area of ΔBCD because of same base, same height.
ΔCDE is the common area to ΔCDF and ΔBCD.

Area of $\Delta DEF = 30 \text{ cm}^2$

Area of $\Delta CDE = 30 \times \frac{30}{20}$
$= 45 \text{ cm}^2$

Area of $\frac{1}{2}$ of rectangle $= 45 + 30$
$= 75 \text{ cm}^2$

$75 - 20 = 55 \text{ cm}^2$

Area of the quadrilateral ADEF is 55 cm^2.

Page 218

16. AB = 3 × 6 = 18 cm
Length of each small rectangle = 18 ÷ 2 = 9 cm
6 + 6 + 6 + 9 + 6 + 9 + 9 + 6 + 9 = 66 cm
The perimeter of rectangle ABCD is 66 cm.

Chapter 13 Practice

Page 225

1. $\frac{1}{4+\frac{1}{5}} = \frac{1}{\frac{20+1}{5}} = \frac{1}{\frac{21}{5}} = \frac{5}{21}$

$\frac{1}{3+\frac{5}{21}} = \frac{1}{\frac{63+5}{21}} = \frac{1}{\frac{68}{21}} = \frac{21}{68}$

$\frac{1}{2+\frac{21}{68}} = \frac{1}{\frac{136+21}{68}} = \frac{1}{\frac{157}{68}} = \frac{68}{157}$

Page 226

2. $\frac{1+\frac{1}{\frac{8-1}{4}}}{1+\frac{1}{\frac{3+1}{3}}} = \frac{1+\frac{1}{\frac{7}{4}}}{1+\frac{1}{\frac{4}{3}}} = \frac{1+\frac{4}{7}}{1+\frac{3}{4}} = \frac{\frac{7+4}{7}}{\frac{4+3}{4}}$

$= \frac{\frac{11}{7}}{\frac{7}{4}} = \frac{11}{7} \times \frac{4}{7} = \frac{44}{49}$

Page 227

3. $\frac{1}{2+\frac{1}{7}} = \frac{1}{\frac{14+1}{7}} = \frac{1}{\frac{15}{7}} = \frac{7}{15}$

$\frac{1}{3-\frac{7}{15}} = \frac{1}{\frac{45-7}{15}} = \frac{1}{\frac{38}{15}} = \frac{15}{38}$

$\frac{1}{4+\frac{15}{38}} = \frac{1}{\frac{152+15}{38}} = \frac{38}{167}$

978-1-62399-075-6
Singapore Math Challenge

Page 228

4. $1 + \frac{1}{3} - (\frac{1}{3} + \frac{1}{4}) + (\frac{1}{4} + \frac{1}{5}) - (\frac{1}{5} + \frac{1}{6})$

$+ (\frac{1}{6} + \frac{1}{7}) - (\frac{1}{7} + \frac{1}{8}) + (\frac{1}{8} + \frac{1}{9})$

$= 1 + \cancel{\frac{1}{3}} - \cancel{\frac{1}{3}} - \cancel{\frac{1}{4}} + \cancel{\frac{1}{5}} - ... + \cancel{\frac{1}{8}} + \frac{1}{9}$

$= 1 + \frac{1}{9}$

$= 1\frac{1}{9}$

Page 229

5. $(1 - \frac{1}{2}) + (1 - \frac{1}{6}) + (1 - \frac{1}{12}) + (1 - \frac{1}{20}) + ... + (1 - \frac{1}{90})$

$= 9 - (\frac{1}{2} + \frac{1}{6} + \frac{1}{12} + \frac{1}{20} + ... + \frac{1}{90})$

$= 9 - (1 - \frac{1}{2} + \frac{1}{2} - \frac{1}{3} + \frac{1}{3} - \frac{1}{4} + \frac{1}{4} - \frac{1}{5} + ... + \frac{1}{9} - \frac{1}{10})$

$= 9 - (1 + \frac{1}{10})$

$= 9 - 1 + \frac{1}{10}$

$= 8\frac{1}{10}$

Page 230

6. $\frac{1}{4} \times (1 - \cancel{\frac{1}{5}} + \cancel{\frac{1}{5}} - \cancel{\frac{1}{9}} + \cancel{\frac{1}{9}} - \cancel{\frac{1}{13}} + ... + \cancel{\frac{1}{97}} - \frac{1}{101})$

$= \frac{1}{4} \times (1 - \frac{1}{101})$

$= \frac{1}{4} \times \frac{100}{101}$

$= \frac{25}{101}$

Page 231

7. *Analysis: Group fractions of the same denominator.*

$\frac{1}{2} + (\frac{1}{3} + \frac{2}{3}) + (\frac{1}{4} + \frac{2}{4} + \frac{3}{4}) + ... + (\frac{1}{10} + ... + \frac{9}{10})$

$= \frac{1}{2} + 1 + 1\frac{1}{2} + 2 + 2\frac{1}{2} + ... + 4\frac{1}{2}$

4 pairs of 5

$2\frac{1}{2}$ is not paired.

$= 4 \times 5 + 2\frac{1}{2}$

$= 20 + 2\frac{1}{2}$

$= 22\frac{1}{2}$

Page 232

8. $\frac{1}{1 \times 3} + \frac{1}{3 \times 5} + \frac{1}{5 \times 7} + ... + \frac{1}{13 \times 15}$ .... (1)

Recall $\frac{1}{n \times (n + d)} = \frac{1}{d} \times (\frac{1}{n} - \frac{1}{n + d})$.

(1) becomes

$\frac{1}{2} \times (1 - \cancel{\frac{1}{3}} + \cancel{\frac{1}{3}} - \cancel{\frac{1}{5}} + \cancel{\frac{1}{5}} - \cancel{\frac{1}{7}} + ... + \cancel{\frac{1}{13}} - \frac{1}{15})$

$= \frac{1}{2} \times (1 - \frac{1}{15})$

$= \frac{1}{2} \times \frac{14}{15}$

$= \frac{14}{30}$

$= \frac{7}{15}$

Page 233

9. Let A be $\frac{1}{2} + \frac{2}{3} + \frac{3}{4} + \frac{4}{5}$.

$$A^2 + \frac{1}{2}A - (1 + A) \times (A - \frac{1}{2})$$

$$= A^2 + \frac{1}{2}A - (A - \frac{1}{2} + A^2 - \frac{1}{2}A)$$

$$= \cancel{A^2} + \cancel{\frac{1}{2}A} - \cancel{A} + \frac{1}{2} - \cancel{A^2} + \cancel{\frac{1}{2}A}$$

$$= \frac{1}{2}$$

Page 234

10. $\frac{2{,}007 + (2{,}007 - 1) \times 2{,}008}{2{,}007 \times 2{,}008 - 1}$

$$= \frac{2{,}007 + 2{,}007 \times 2{,}008 - 2{,}008}{2{,}007 \times 2{,}008 - 1}$$

$$= \frac{2{,}007 \times 2{,}008 - 2{,}008 + 2{,}007}{2{,}007 \times 2{,}008 - 1}$$

$$= \frac{2{,}007 \times 2{,}008 - 1}{2{,}007 \times 2{,}008 - 1}$$

$$= 1$$

Page 235

11. $\frac{1}{2{,}008} + \frac{2}{2{,}008} + \frac{3}{2{,}008} + ... + \frac{2{,}006}{2{,}008} + \frac{2{,}007}{2{,}008}$

$$= \frac{1 + 2 + 3 + ... + 2{,}006 + 2{,}007}{2{,}008}$$

Using the formula:

$$\frac{(\text{1st no.} + \text{last no.}) \times \text{how many numbers}}{2}$$

$$= \frac{(\cancel{1 + 2{,}007}) \times 2{,}007}{2 \times \cancel{2{,}008}}$$

$$= 1{,}003.5$$

Page 236

12. Except for the first and the last fractions, the rest are grouped in fours:

$$\frac{2}{2{,}007} - \frac{3}{2{,}007} - \frac{4}{2{,}007} + \frac{5}{2{,}007} = 0$$

$$\frac{6}{2{,}007} - \frac{7}{2{,}007} - \frac{8}{2{,}007} + \frac{9}{2{,}007} = 0$$

$$\vdots$$

$$\frac{2{,}002}{2{,}007} - \frac{2{,}003}{2{,}007} - \frac{2{,}004}{2{,}007} + \frac{2{,}005}{2{,}007} = 0$$

$$= \frac{1}{2{,}007} + 0 + 0 + ... + 0 + \frac{2{,}006}{2{,}007}$$

$$= 1$$

Page 237

13. $\frac{2{,}000}{1 \times 2} + \frac{2{,}000}{2 \times 3} + \frac{2{,}000}{3 \times 4} + ... + \frac{2{,}000}{1{,}999 \times 2{,}000}$

$$= 2{,}000 \times (\frac{1}{1 \times 2} + \frac{1}{2 \times 3} + \frac{1}{3 \times 4} ... + \frac{1}{1{,}999 \times 2{,}000})$$

$$= 2{,}000 \times (1 - \frac{1}{2} + \frac{1}{2} - \frac{1}{3} + \frac{1}{3} - \frac{1}{4} + ... + \frac{1}{1{,}999} - \frac{1}{2{,}000})$$

$$= 2{,}000 \times (1 - \frac{1}{2{,}000})$$

$$= 2{,}000 \times \frac{1{,}999}{2{,}000}$$

$$= 1{,}999$$

978-1-62399-075-6
Singapore Math Challenge

Page 238

14. As in question 11, use the formula for each denominator.

$$\frac{1}{1+2} + \frac{1}{1+2+3} + \frac{1}{1+2+3+4} + \dots + \frac{1}{1+2+3+\dots+50}$$

$$= \frac{1}{\frac{(1+2)\times 2}{2}} + \frac{1}{\frac{(1+3)\times 3}{2}} + \frac{1}{\frac{(1+4)\times 4}{2}} + \dots + \frac{1}{\frac{(1+50)\times 50}{2}}$$

$$= \frac{2}{2\times 3} + \frac{2}{3\times 4} + \frac{2}{4\times 5} + \dots + \frac{2}{50\times 51}$$

$$= 2\times(\frac{1}{2} - \frac{1}{3} + \frac{1}{3} - \frac{1}{4} + \frac{1}{4} - \frac{1}{5} + \dots + \frac{1}{50} - \frac{1}{51})$$

$$= 2\times(\frac{1}{2} - \frac{1}{51})$$

$$= 2\times\frac{51-2}{102}$$

$$= \frac{49}{51}$$

Chapter 14 Practice

Page 246

1. **(a)** No square number ends with 7.
(b) No square number ends with 8.
(c) 15 × 15 = 225 is not correct since digits in the tens and hundreds places should be different.
25 × 25 = 625
(d) 14 × 14 = 196

Page 247

2. **(a)** The last digit of the number must be 3 or 7.
43 × 43 = 1,849
47 × 47 = 2,209
2,209 is a square number.
(b) 3,402 is not a square number as it ends with 2.
(c) The last digit must be 6.
3,136 = 56 × 56
3,136 is a square number.
(d) The last digit must be 1 or 9.
69 × 69 = 4,761
71 × 71 = 5,041
5,041 is a square number.

Page 248

3. 1 × 1 = 1
2 × 2 = 4
3 × 3 = 9
4 × 4 = 16
5 × 5 = 25
6 × 6 = 36
7 × 7 = 49
8 × 8 = 64
9 × 9 = 81
10 × 10 = 100
The other numbers that can occur in the ones place of a square number are 4, 5, 6 and 9.

978-1-62399-075-6
Singapore Math Challenge

Page 249

4. $17 \times 17 = 289$
$18 \times 18 = 324$ ✓
$19 \times 19 = 361$ ✓
$20 \times 20 = 400$ ✓
$21 \times 21 = 441$ ✓
$22 \times 22 = 484$ ✓
$23 \times 23 = 529$
The square numbers that are larger than 300 but smaller than 500 are 324, 361, 400, 441 and 484.

Page 250

5. 2,100 — ⑦ — 300 — ② — 150 — ② — 75 — ⑤ — 15 — ③ — ⑤

$2,100 = 2 \times 2 \times 3 \times 5 \times 5 \times 7$
$2,100 \times m = 2 \times 2 \times 3 \times ③ \times 5 \times 5 \times 7 \times ⑦$
$m = 3 \times 7 = 21$
The smallest possible value of m is 21.

Page 251

6. 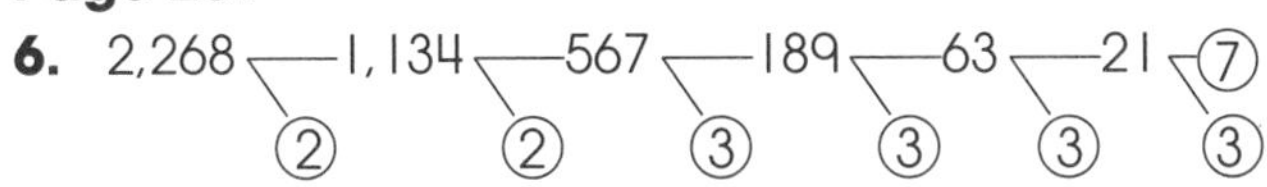

$2,268 = 2 \times 2 \times 3 \times 3 \times 3 \times 3 \times 7$
$2,268 \times$ David's age $= 2 \times 2 \times 3 \times 3 \times 3 \times 3 \times 7 \times ⑦$
David's age = 7
David's father's age $= 2 \times 2 \times 3 \times 3 = 36$
David's grandfather's age $= 3 \times 3 \times 7 = 63$
David's grandfather is 63 years old, David's father is 36 years old and David is 7 years old.

Page 252

7. 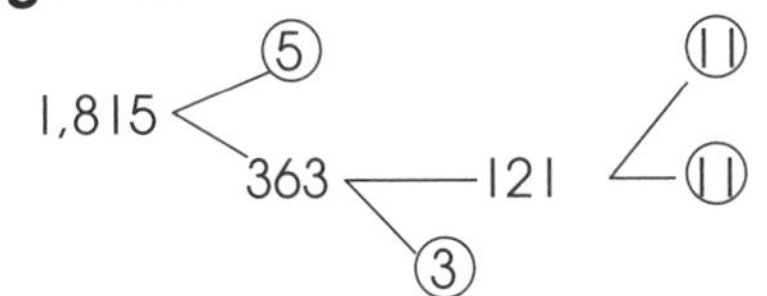

$1,815 = 3 \times 5 \times 11 \times 11$
$1,815 \times m = 3 \times ③ \times 5 \times ⑤ \times 11 \times 11 = 15$
The smallest possible value of m is 15.

Page 253

8. Make a list of square numbers.
1, 4, 9, 16, ㉕, ㊱, 49, 64, (81), ...
Using guess-and-check method,
$142 = 25 + 36 + 81$
$25 = 5 \times 5$ $36 = 6 \times 6$ $81 = 9 \times 9$
The sides of each square are 6 cm, 9 cm and 5 cm respectively.

Page 254

9. Make a list of square numbers.
+3 +5 +7 +9 +11 +13 +15
1, 4, 9, 16, 25, 36, 49, 64, ...
$101 - 3 = 98$
$98 \div 2 = 49$
$49 + 1 = 50$
$50 \times 50 = 2,500$
The number of students in the year 2005 was 2,500.
$50 + 1 = 51$
$51 \times 51 = 2,601$
The number of students in the year 2006 was 2,601.

Page 255, 256

10. (a)

Power of 6	6^1	6^2	6^3	6^4	...	...	...
Ones digit	6	6	6	6	...	...	...

The value of the ones digit of 26^{62} is 6.

(b)

Power of 3	3^1	3^2	3^3	3^4	3^5	3^6	3^7	3^8	...
Ones digit	3	9	7	1	3	9	7	1	...
					R1	R2	R3	R0	

$303 \div 4 = 75$ R 3
The value of the ones digit of 33^{303} is 7.

(c)

Power of 4	4^1	4^2	4^3	4^4	4^5	4^6	...	...
Ones digit	4	6	4	6	4	6	...	...
					R1	R0		

$15 \div 2 = 7$ R 1
The value of the ones digit of 124^{15} is 4.

(d)

Power of 9	9^1	9^2	9^3	9^4	...	...
Ones digit	9	1	9	1	...	...
			R1	R0		

$91 \div 2 = 45$ R 1
The value of the ones digit of 19^{91} is 9.

978-1-62399-075-6
Singapore Math Challenge

Page 257, 258

11. (a)

Power of 2	2^1	2^2	2^3	2^4	2^5	2^6	2^7	2^8	...
Last digit	2	4	8	6	2	4	8	6	...
					R1	R2	R3	R0	

$30 \div 4 = 7$ R 2
The value of the last digit of 2^{30} is 4.

(b)

Power of 3	3^1	3^2	3^3	3^4	3^5	3^6	3^7	3^8	...	...
Last digit	3	9	7	1	3	9	7	1	...	...
					R1	R2	R3	R0		

$2,000 \div 4 = 500$ R 0
The value of the last digit of $3^{2,000}$ is 1.

(c)

Power of 7	7^1	7^2	7^3	7^4	7^5	7^6	7^7	7^8	...
Last digit	7	9	3	1	7	9	3	1	...
					R1	R2	R3	R0	

$2,002 \div 4 = 500$ R 2
The value of the last digit of $7^{2,002}$ is 9.

(d)

Power of 9	9^1	9^2	9^3	9^4	...	...
Last digit	9	1	9	1	...	...
			R1	R0		

$99 \div 2 = 49$ R 1
The value of the last digit of 99^{99} is 9.

Page 259

12. (a) $27^{2,000}$

Power of 7	7^1	7^2	7^3	7^4	7^5	7^6	7^7	7^8	...
Ones digit	7	9	3	1	7	9	3	1	...
					R1	R2	R3	R0	

$2,000 \div 4 = 500$ R 0
The value of the ones digit of $27^{2,000}$ is 1.

(b) $2^{216,091} - 1$
2, 4, 8, 6, 2, 4, 8, 6, ...
R1 R2 R3 R0
$216,091 \div 4 = 54,022$ R 3
The value of the ones digit of $2^{216,091}$ is 8.
$8 - 1 = 7$
The value of the ones digit in $2^{216,091} - 1$ is 7.

Page 260

13. $9 \times 1 \times 3 \times 5 \times 7$
ones digit = 5
$0 \times 2 \times 4 \times 6$
ones digit = 0
$5 - 0 = 5$
The value of the ones digit is 5.

Page 261

14. For 78^{87}

Power of 8	8^1	8^2	8^3	8^4	8^5	8^6	8^7	8^8	...
Ones digit	8	4	2	6	8	4	2	6	...
					R1	R2	R3	R0	

$87 \div 4 = 21$ R 3
The value of the ones digit of 78^{87} is 2.
For 87^{78}

Power of 7	7^1	7^2	7^3	7^4	7^5	7^6	7^7	7^8	...
Ones digit	7	9	3	1	7	9	3	1	...
					R1	R2	R3	R0	

$78 \div 4 = 19$ R 2
The value of the ones digit of 87^{78} is 9.
$2 + 9 = 11$
The sum of the values of the ones digits of 78^{87} and 87^{78} is 11.

Page 262

15. $1,001 \div 11 = 91$
1,001 1,001 ... 1,001 1,001 $\div$ 11
(1,001 times)
= 9,100 9,100 ... 0,091
The remainder will be 0 when such a number is divided by 11.

Page 263

16. $2 \times 5 = 10$
Each pair of (2, 5) gives a zero.
There are more 2s than 5s in
$1 \times 2 \times 3 \times ... \times 99 \times 100$.
It is enough to find the number of 5s.
The 1st set of 5:
5, 10, 15, 20, ..., 100 (20 in all)
The 2nd set of 5:
25, 50, 75, 100 (4 in all)
$20 + 4 = 24$
There are 24 consecutive zeros.

978-1-62399-075-6
Singapore Math Challenge

Page 264

17. There is no change in the ones digits of 1^{5}, 5^{32}, 6^{25} and 10^{41}.
The ones digits of 2^{9}, 3^{13}, 4^{17}, 7^{29}, 8^{33} and 9^{37} are the same as those of 2^{1}, 3^{1}, 4^{1}, 7^{1}, 8^{1} and 9^{1}.
$1 + 2 + 3 + 4 + ... + 9 = 45$
The ones digit is 5.

Page 265

18. For $10! = 1 \times 2 \times 3 \times ... \times 10$, the last 2 digits are 00.
The same goes for 11!, 12!, ..., 99!.
This is because there will always be 2 or more pairs of (2, 5).
The sum of the last 2 digits in
$1! + 2! + ... 9!$
is $1 + 2 + 6 + 24 + 20 + 20 + 40 + 20 + 80 = 213$
The last 2 digits in the expression are 13.

Chapter 15 Practice

Page 273

1. Number of 3s: 2
Number of 1s: 2
Number of 5s: 2
Total number of digits: 10
$\frac{2 + 2 + 2}{10} \times 100\% = 60\%$
The three digits have a 60% appearance.

Page 274

2. Compare year 2007 with 2006.
$\frac{3,500 - 2,500}{2,500} \times 100\% = \frac{1,000}{2,500} \times 100\%$
$= 40\%$
Compare year 2009 with 2008.
$\frac{6,000 - 4,500}{4,500} \times 100\% = \frac{1,500}{4,500} \times 100\%$
$= 33.3\%$
Compare year 2012 with 2011.
$\frac{10,000 - 8,000}{8,000} \times 100\% = \frac{2,000}{8,000} \times 100\%$
$= 25\%$
The sharpest increase is in the year 2007.

Page 275

3. Original area: $10 \times 10 = 100\ cm^2$
New area: $13 \times 13 = 169\ cm^2$
$\frac{169 - 100}{100} \times 100\% = 69\%$
The increase is 69%.

Page 276

4. ***Method 1: Use Drawing***

The volume of ice decreases by $\frac{1}{11}$ when it melts completely to water.

$\frac{1}{11} \times 100\% = 9\frac{1}{11}\%$

Method 2: Use Reasoning

Volume of water → 100%
Volume of ice → 110%

It decreases by

$1 - \frac{100}{110} = \frac{1}{11}$ when it melts completely to water.

$\frac{1}{11} \times 100\% = 9\frac{1}{11}\%$

The volume of ice decreases by $9\frac{1}{11}\%$ after it melts completely to water again.

Page 277

5. Let the sales volume be 100% in year 1.

$100\% \times (1 + \frac{20}{100}) = 120\%$ in year 2

$120\% \times (1 + \frac{30}{100}) = 156\%$ in year 3

$156\% \times (1 - \frac{25}{100}) = 156 \times \frac{3}{4}$

$= 117\%$ in year 4

$117\% - 100\% = 17\%$

The sales in year 4 increase by 17% compared to year 1.

Page 278

6. $56{,}000 \times \frac{45}{100} = 25{,}200$

$56{,}000 - 25{,}200 = 30{,}800$

A and B should get \$25,200 and \$30,800 respectively.

Page 279

7. Let what Benny has be 100%.

Alice has 120% and Celine has 75%.

100% + 120% + 75% = 295%

295% → \$590

5% → \$10

120% − 75% = 45%

45% → \$90

Alice has \$90 more compared to Celine.

Page 280

8. 80 × 20% = \$16 goes to books and entertainment.

80 − 16 = \$64 is left

By guess and check,

\$30 → food
\$10 → transportation
\$24 → savings

$\frac{24}{80} \times 100 = 30\%$

30% of his money goes to savings.

Page 281

9. 400 − 250 = 150

670 − 150 = 520

Transfer 150 white beads from B to A.

A now has 400 black beads and 400 white beads.

A	B
400 black	200 black
400 white	520 white

200 − 40 = 160

520 − 40 = 480

160 : 480 + 160 = 1 : 4

40 black beads and 190 white beads must be transferred from B to A.

Page 282

10. The selling price of a basketball is
$40 \times (1 + 20\%) = \$48$
Let there be f number of footballs.
$$40 \times f + 48 \times (f + 15) = 5{,}000 + 1{,}000$$
$$40f + 48f + 720 = 6{,}000$$
$$88f = 5{,}280$$
$$f = 60$$
There are 60 footballs.

Page 283

11. $\frac{72}{360} = \frac{36}{180} = \frac{2}{10}$
$\frac{2}{10} \times 100\% = 20\%$
There are 20% Indians and 20% Europeans.
$\frac{162}{360} = \frac{81}{180} = \frac{9}{20}$
$\frac{9}{20} \times 100\% = 45\%$
There are 45% Indonesians.
$100 - 45 - 20 - 20 = 15\%$
There are 15% Chinese.
$20\% - 15\% = 5\%$
$5\% \rightarrow 100{,}000$
$45\% \rightarrow 900{,}000$
There are 900,000 Indonesians.

Page 284

12. Let the number of boys be b.
$$1.2 \times b + (2{,}000 - b) \times 0.8 = 0.96 \times 2{,}000$$
$$1.2 \times b + 1{,}600 - 0.8 \times b = 1{,}920$$
$$0.4 \times b = 1{,}920 - 1{,}600$$
$$= 320$$
$$b = 800$$
$800 \times 1.2 = 960$
There are 960 boys in the school this year.

Page 285

13. $40 \times 0.8 = \$32$
$6 \times 3 = \$18$ on apples
$32 - 18 = \$14$ dollars left
$14 + 2 = \$16$ needed
$\frac{2}{16} \times 100\% = 12.5\%$
The discount on the bananas is 12.5%.

Page 286

14. Let the number of DVDs bought in 1st week be d.
The number of DVDs bought in 2nd week is 2d.
$(\frac{24 \times d}{4} + \frac{25 \times 2d}{5}) \times 120\%$
$= (6d + 10d) \times 1.2$
$= 19.2d$
Let k be the price of each pack of 3 DVDs.
$k \times \frac{3d}{3} = k \times d$
Equating,
$k \times \not{d} = 19.2\not{d}$
$k = 19.2$
Each pack of 3 DVDs was sold for \$19.20.

978-1-62399-075-6
Singapore Math Challenge

Chapter 16 Practice

Page 296

1.

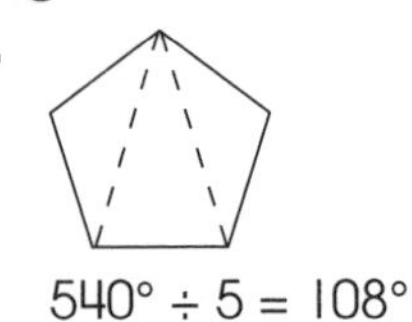

There are 3 triangles.
Total interior angles
$= 3 \times 180$
$= 540°$

$540° \div 5 = 108°$

Page 297

2.

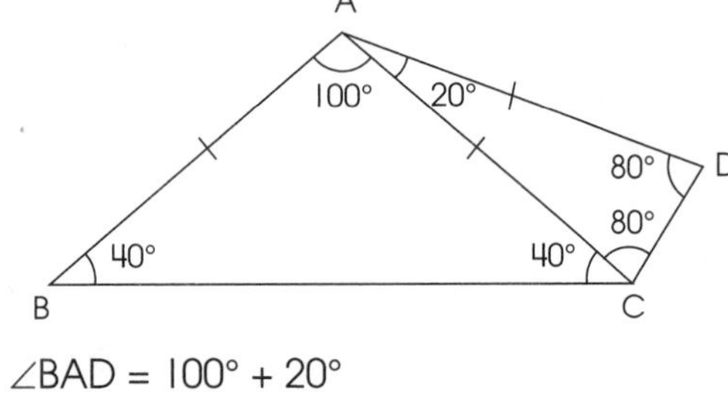

$\angle BAD = 100° + 20°$
$= 120°$

Page 298

3.

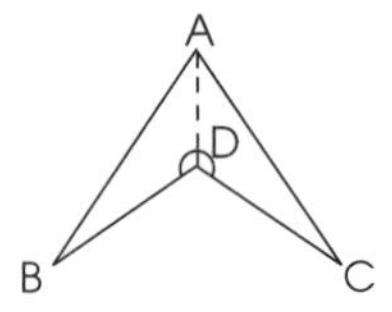

Divide the figure into 2 triangles.
$\angle A + \angle B + \angle C + \angle D$
$= 2 \times 180°$
$= 360°$

Page 299

4. For $\triangle BCE$,

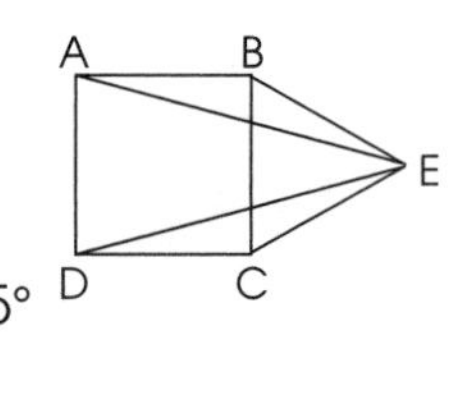

$\angle B = \angle C = \angle E = 60°$
$\angle ABE = 90° + 60° = 150°$
$\angle BEA = \angle CED$
$= (180° - 150°) \div 2 = 15°$
$\angle AED = 60° - 15° - 15°$
$= 30°$

Page 300

5.

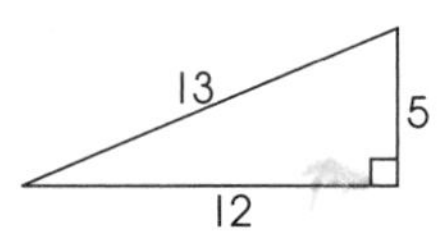

$\angle 1 = 180° - (\angle a + \angle b)$
$\angle 2 = 180° - (\angle c + \angle d)$
$\angle 3 = \angle 3'$
$= 180° - (\angle e + \angle f)$
$\angle 1 + \angle 2 + \angle 3' = 180°$
$180° - (\angle a + \angle b) + 180° - (\angle c + \angle d)$
$+ 180° - (\angle e + \angle f)$
$= 180°$
$540° - (\angle a + \angle b + \angle c + \angle d + \angle e + \angle f)$
$= 180°$
Clearly,
$\angle a + \angle b + \angle c + \angle d + \angle e + \angle f = 360°$

Page 301

6. Recall the Pythagorean Triples given in Concept 4.
(3, 4, 5), (5, 12, 13), (6, 8, 10), ...
$30 = 5 + 12 + 13$

13, 5, 12

Area of the $\Delta = \frac{1}{2} \times 12 \times 5$
$= 30 \text{ cm}^2$
The longest side is 13 cm.

978-1-62399-075-6
Singapore Math Challenge

Page 302

7.

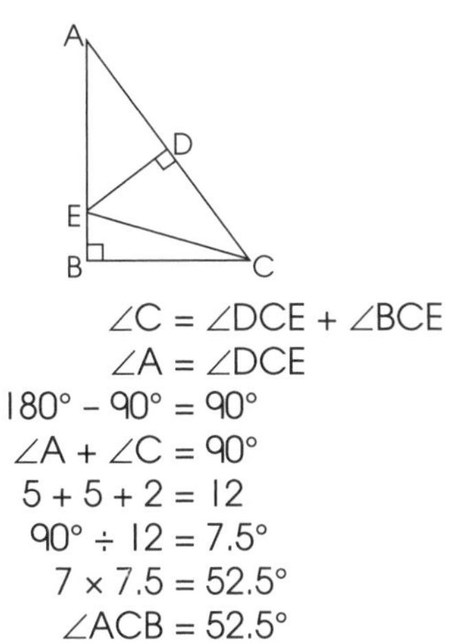

$\angle C = \angle DCE + \angle BCE$
$\angle A = \angle DCE$
$180° - 90° = 90°$
$\angle A + \angle C = 90°$
$5 + 5 + 2 = 12$
$90° \div 12 = 7.5°$
$7 \times 7.5 = 52.5°$
$\angle ACB = 52.5°$

Page 303

8.

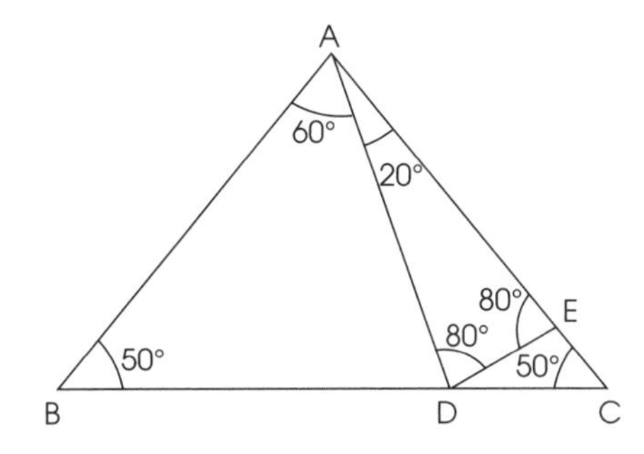

Suppose $\angle DAE = 20°$
$\angle BAC = 60° + 20° = 80°$
$\angle ABC = \angle ACB$
$= (180° - 80°) \div 2 = 50°$
$\angle ADE = \angle AED = 80°$
$\angle CDE + \angle DCE = 80°$
$\angle DCE = 50°$
$\angle CDE = 80° - 50° = 30°$
The result is still 30° if we assume $\angle DAE$ to be 30° or 40°.

Page 304

9.

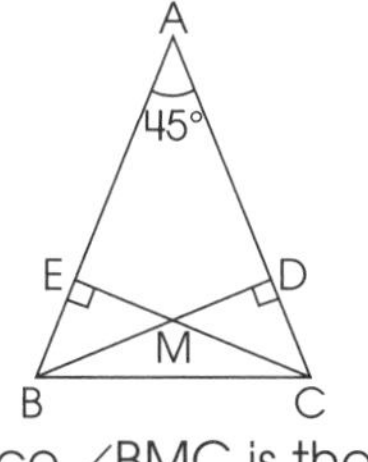

$\angle ADB = \angle BEC = 90°$
$\angle ABD = 45°$
$\angle BMC = \angle BEM + \angle EBM$ since $\angle BMC$ is the exterior angle
$= 90° + 45°$
$= 135°$

Page 305

10.

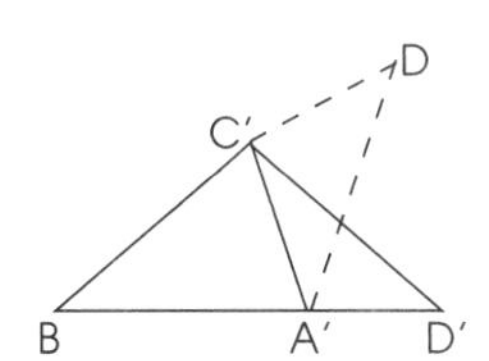

Cut along AC and paste ΔACD as shown.
$A'B = A'D$
$\angle A'BC' = \angle D = 40°$
$\angle C'A'B = 70°$
$\angle C'A'D' = 110°$
$\angle A'C'D' = 180° - 110° - 40°$
$= 30°$

Page 306

11.

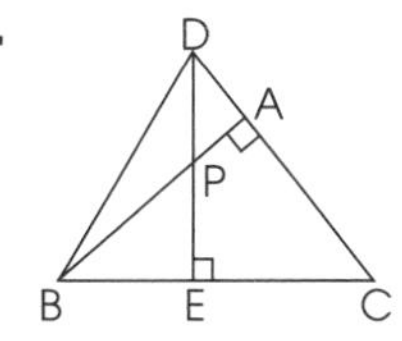

$\angle BPE = 50° = \angle APD$ (opposite angles)
$\angle BPD = \angle APE = 180° - 50° = 130°$
Sum of interior angles of APEC is $2 \times 180° = 360°$.
$\angle C = 360° - 90° - 90° - 130° = 50°$

Page 307

12.

$2 + 3 + 4 = 9$

$360° \div 9 = 40°$

$2 \times 40° = 80$

$3 \times 40° = 120°$

$4 \times 40° = 160°$

The 3 interior angles are

$180° - 80° = 100°$

$180° - 120° = 60°$

$180° - 160° = 20°$

$100° : 60° : 20° = 5 : 3 : 1$

Page 308

13.

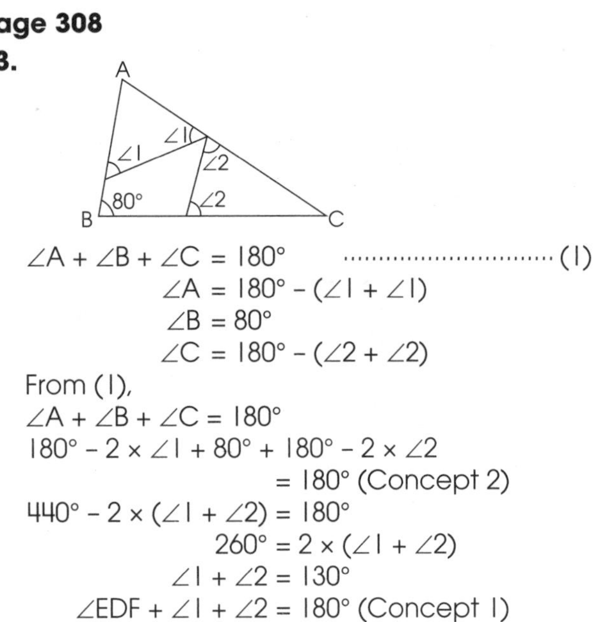

$\angle A + \angle B + \angle C = 180°$ .... (1)

$\angle A = 180° - (\angle 1 + \angle 1)$

$\angle B = 80°$

$\angle C = 180° - (\angle 2 + \angle 2)$

From (1),

$\angle A + \angle B + \angle C = 180°$

$180° - 2 \times \angle 1 + 80° + 180° - 2 \times \angle 2$

$= 180°$ (Concept 2)

$440° - 2 \times (\angle 1 + \angle 2) = 180°$

$260° = 2 \times (\angle 1 + \angle 2)$

$\angle 1 + \angle 2 = 130°$

$\angle EDF + \angle 1 + \angle 2 = 180°$ (Concept 1)

$\angle EDF = 50°$

Page 309

14.

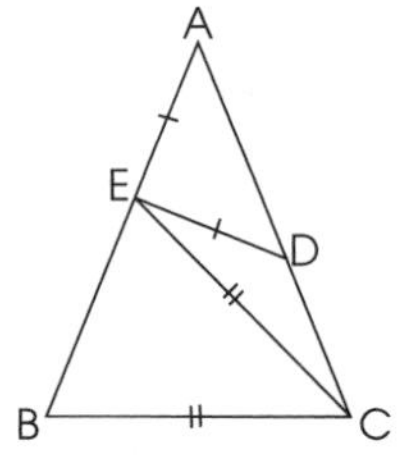

$\angle CED = \angle DCE$ (isosceles Δ)

$\angle A = \angle ADE$ (isosceles Δ)

$\angle ADE = \angle CED + \angle DCE$

(sum of 2 opposite interior angles)

$\angle DCE = \frac{1}{2}ADE = \frac{1}{2}\angle A$

$\angle BEC = \angle DCE + \angle A$

(sum of 2 opposite interior angles)

$= \frac{1}{2}\angle A + \angle A$

$= \frac{3}{2}\angle A$

Similarly,

$\angle B = \frac{3}{2}\angle A$ (isosceles Δ)

$\angle A + \angle B + \angle C = 180°$

$\angle A + \frac{3}{2}\angle A + \frac{3}{2}\angle A = 180°$

$4\angle A = 180°$

$\angle A = 45°$